بسم الله الرحمن الرحيم

IV Publishing
Email: sales@islamicvillage.co.uk
Website: www.islamicvillage.co.uk

Distributed by HUbooks
Email: info@hubooks.com
Website: www.hubooks.com

Title: Introduction to the Principles of Qur'ānic Exegesis
Translator: Moṣṭafā al-Badawī

Arabic Title: Al-Madkhal ilā Uṣūl al-Tafsīr
Original Author: Usama al-Sayyid Mahmud al-Azhari
Published by: Al-Wābil al-Ṣayyib, 7047 Al-Mokattam Street,
Cairo, Egypt (First Edition - 2010CE)

ISBN: 978-0-9520853-2-4

Cover Design: Faadil

OUTSTANDING

Designed, printed & bound in the United Kingdom by OUTSTANDING
Email: books@outstanding-media.co.uk Tel: +44 (0)121 327 3277

INTRODUCTION
to the
Principles
of
Qur'ānic
EXEGESIS

Usama al-Sayyid
Mahmud al-Azhari

*Translated from arabic with
introduction and notes by*

Mostafa al-Badawi

ISLAMIC·VILLAGE

Contents

TRANSLATOR'S INTRODUCTION 9

PREFACE 15

PRINCIPLE ONE OF QUR'ĀNIC EXEGESIS 19

The influence of the relation between the Qur'ān and the various sciences on defining the tools and resources of the exegete

PRINCIPLE TWO OF QUR'ĀNIC EXEGESIS 29

The levels of Qur'ānic guidance and their influence on the exegete's understanding of the Qur'ān's universal address

PRINCIPLE THREE OF QUR'ĀNIC EXEGESIS 37

The Qur'ān explains itself

PRINCIPLE FOUR OF QUR'ĀNIC EXEGESIS 41

The Prophet's *Sunna* is the second of the two Revelations, its source is the Qur'ān and it is the explanation of its meanings

PRINCIPLE FIVE OF QUR'ĀNIC EXEGESIS 47

The exegete must acquaint himself with the Science of the Principles of Jurisprudence, because it contains important rules for understanding the text and analyzing it

PRINCIPLE SIX OF QUR'ĀNIC EXEGESIS 51

The need of the exegete to keep up with the amplifications in the meanings of verbal expressions that accompany the expansion of the limits of knowledge of a given civilization and the cumulative effects of its experiences

PRINCIPLE SEVEN OF QUR'ĀNIC EXEGESIS 57

The effects of grasping the various manners in which the Qur'ān affects the soul on understanding and analyzing the text, and the necessity of learning that method

PRINCIPLE EIGHT OF QUR'ĀNIC EXEGESIS 63

The stories of the Prophets are expositions of the various cognitive styles governing humans throughout history

PRINCIPLE NINE OF QUR'ĀNIC EXEGESIS 67

The axes of the various sūras of the Qur'ān and their influence on understanding the text

PRINCIPLE TEN OF QUR'ĀNIC EXEGESIS 71

Fundamental principles of the Qur'ān or independent inference: a practical method applied by the community over the centuries to derive benefit from the verses of the Qur'ān

PRINCIPLE ELEVEN OF QUR'ĀNIC EXEGESIS 83

Divine existential laws governing human societies permeate the Book and form the subject of one of the essential sciences of the Qur'ān

PRINCIPLE TWELVE OF QUR'ĀNIC EXEGESIS 87

The Science of Qur'ānic Purposes, one of the most important tools of the exegete

PRINCIPLE THIRTEEN OF QUR'ĀNIC EXEGESIS 93

Effect of the Science of Derivatives on understanding the text

Translator's Introduction

THE ART OF Qur'ānic commentary or exegesis is one of the most essential branches of Islamic knowledge, because the Qur'ān is the primary source of knowledge for all Muslims. Since the Qur'ān is generally considered to be a synthetic whole capable of generating by analysis everything that the Muslim community will ever need, a thorough understanding of its text is an essential requirement for experts in all fields of Islamic knowledge. The process of understanding the Qur'ān comprises two components: the first is more or less static, involving as it were immutable truths, while the second is dynamic, involving the application of Qur'ānic knowledge to deal with ever changing social and historical situations, as well as new scientific discoveries. It is thus a process that needs to keep up with changing circumstances by constant renewal. Therefore, to be able to complete their work successfully, the commentators or exegetes of every age are required to arm themselves with every resource available in their time. The resources necessary for our times are evidently different from those required in previous centuries. If they are to be used, these resources need first to be identified and delineated. This is what drove the author of this book to act on the suggestion of the former Grand Muftī of Egypt, Shaykh ʿAlī Jumʿa, to compile in a single work the gist of everything that has been said by previous scholars, and then add to it the novel ideas which are in the process of being formulated by contemporary scholars, including Shaykh ʿAlī himself and the author.

A compact text of this kind is addressed primarily to professional scholars and prospective exegetes, which is why on first reading I found it difficult. Nevertheless, struck by how vitally important the topic was, I suggested that the book be translated to English, while declining to do it myself, my excuse being a chronic lack of time. However, many months later, at the insistence of the author, Shaykh Usāma, I finally agreed to undertake the translation, but on condition that he give us a series of four lectures on the book, which he graciously did. The sessions proved richly productive; we asked many questions and digressed into many related and unrelated topics. Any word or passage I found obscure or ambiguous was inquired about and clarified. Translation being a kind of interpretation, the liberties I felt obliged to take with the text to make it more accessible to the English reader were repeatedly discussed with the author and his approval obtained. I hope that following his explanatory efforts the English text will be sufficiently clear and require no more than the few brief notes I have added here and there.

The author, a teacher of Islamic sciences at the illustrious Azhar University in Cairo, is in possession of a profound grasp of the traditional scholarly sciences, as well as being fully conversant with the cultural, sociological and historical conditions of the times.

Notwithstanding the above statement that the work is aimed at professional scholars, there is a lot of precious information to be gained from reading it. This is especially true for those who, while not professional scholars, nevertheless wish to acquaint themselves with the difficulties and intricacies of Qur'ānic exegesis and thus be able to more fully appreciate the various commentaries they have at hand.

Some of the subjects mentioned by the author have already been discussed by previous writers; others seem to be new additions demanded by the conditions of our times. These will require future in-depth exploration by contemporary and future scholars.

The book is composed of thirteen chapters, each concerned with one of the principles of exegesis as conceived by the author.

Principles One and Two serve, together with the preface, as a general introduction to the basics of the subject.

Principles Three and Four are concomitant. They state that the primary means of understanding the Qur'ān is the Qur'ān itself, followed by the Prophet's *Sunna*. This indeed is the basic procedure that exegetes have always followed; to understand any particular topic in the Qur'ān, they must start by compiling the verses connected with it and comparing them with each other, then connecting the relevant Prophetic traditions or *ḥadīths*, and then compiling the comments of the Companions, especially those of Ibn 'Abbās, then those of the Followers[1], and finally those of subsequent scholars and men of God if needed. This is generally accompanied by a linguistic analysis of key terms. How much of this material is actually quoted in any particular commentary depends on the intended length of the work, some commentaries being detailed and comprehensive, others quite brief. The length of the text and the creed and philosophical orientation of the exegete will dictate what other avenues of exploration will be pursued: for instance, historical information from Muslim sources, and stories of previous communities from Jewish and other sources.

Principle Ten, which is that of inferences understood independently

1 The Companions are those of the Prophet - may God's blessings and peace be upon him - who are those who saw him, even once, and died as Muslims. The Followers are the generation following the Companions, their students.

from the context, has also been agreed upon since the first exegetes.

Principle Six, which states that the exegete must be familiar with the latest that the civilization of his time has produced in terms of knowledge, has also always been known; witness for instance the monumental commentary of Rāzī[2] where he makes use of practically every science known to mankind in his days. However, this principle needs to be stressed in our age, where the expansion of knowledge is explosive and the use of new data needs to be strictly regulated according to explicit criteria which restrict the exegete to the incontrovertible scientific facts of the age, in order to avoid theories still at the stage of experimentation or research.

Similarly, principles Twelve and Thirteen, which are those of Qur'ānic purposes and the Science of Derivatives, have been known since the old days, but need to be given renewed attention and used in a more systematic manner. We have yet to draw the full benefit of their potentials.

Principles Eight, Nine and Eleven are entirely novel approaches to understanding the Qur'ān. The stories of the Prophets are here considered as prototypal expositions of the various manners in which humanity has responded in the past to essential issues such as the existence of God, revelation, right and wrong, and the relation between religion and life in general and politics in particular. Humanity being what it is, we expect it to continue responding in the same manner in the future, so that the teachings here remain as relevant today as they were fourteen centuries ago. Next, the concept is suggested of the presence within each *sūra* of an axis governing the variety of ideas discussed in it. Identifying and defining these

2 Imām Fakhr al-Dīn al-Rāzī. His *Tafsīr* is entitled *Mafātīh al-Ghayb*. He died in 606 A.H.

axes would obviously allow a more strategic and thus coherent comprehension of the text. Finally, the laws can be identified that govern human societies and the rise and fall of civilizations, which would help to create a Science of Civilization based on revelation.

The author presented the results of his efforts to Shaykh ʿAlī Jumʿa, who was very pleased with it. The whole text was included, before being published separately, as an additional introduction to the first volume of Shaykh ʿAlī's own Qur'ānic commentary.[3]

All the notes are mine, except for the references and note 6 on page 26.

3 *Al-Nibrās fī Tafsīr al-Qur'ān al-Karīm*, Shaykh ʿAlī Jumʿa, al-Wābil al-Ṣayyib, Cairo, 1431 A.H., 2009 C.E.

Preface

ALL PRAISE BELONGS to God, Lord of all beings. May blessings and peace be upon our master the Messenger of God, the best of God's creation, and upon his Family, Companions, and all those who support and follow his guidance till Judgment Day.

To proceed: The Noble Qur'ān is a divine book, a sacred text, originated from God. It includes what He saw fit in the way of beliefs, legal rulings, good manners, organizational guidelines, and narratives. It was His will – Transcendent is He – that it should have a miraculous nature, way beyond human capability. Unlike other divine books, He took it upon Himself to preserve it because it is the final and all-comprehending divine address to mankind, containing the principles of divine guidance and the essence of all previous divine messages. It was meant to be flexible and open-ended so that it can be addressed to the humanity of all times and places, unlike previous scriptures which were intended for specific circumstances, so that they were closed systems, even while preparing the ground for the greatest guidance of all that is the Qur'ān.

The general and particular purposes of the Qur'ān revolve around four major axes: Instruction, guidance, miraculousness, and legal rules.

•

The first, instruction, is the exposition of the subject of divinity, providing proof of its truth, teaching the attributes and perfection of the true Deity, explaining clearly His purpose in creating this universe and His relationship to His creation, namely to create and to command; and of that command is Revelation. Instruction clarifies how He created man for noble purposes, how to understand man's function in this life, and the resources and capabilities granted him by God to enable him to achieve these purposes, before finally clarifying his end state in the next world. It also clarifies what constitutes the overall framework of the Islamic cognitive model upon which depend Islam's value system, what the behavioural implications of such a model are, how the various sciences and branches of knowledge that were born of these premises are generated, and how they are capable of realizing these objects.

•

The second, guidance, is the method the Qur'ān uses in addressing created beings, the manner in which it approaches the above mentioned subjects, and its subtlety in diversifying its approaches to make these realities accessible to people's minds. Guidance includes the various techniques and strategies used to prove a point, discuss, refute and convince, while choosing formulations suited to the psychology of the recipient. Among these are the use of promises and threats, arousing desire, evoking the universal principles that people of all denominations acknowledge, showing how these confirm the realities in the Qur'ān, stimulating reflection and opening up the door for rational inquiry.

•

The third, the miraculous quality, is a reality which, while being difficult to define, suffuses the whole Book with order, harmony, and awe-inspiring dignity; the end result is an extraordinarily impressive style carrying a message that transcends time and place. In addition to the explicit, astounding challenge of its miraculous quality, the text possesses the quality of being able to meet changing circumstances with ever-renewed meanings.

•

The fourth, legal rules, consist in a precise description of the various situations and kinds of behaviour that responsible beings[1] are liable to, and their consequences in this world and the next. They also include counsels and orders, the imposition of certain rules and the manner in which the various aspects of each individual life can be evaluated and remoulded. Lastly, it includes the laws and conditions regulating human interaction, which cover all areas of human activity.

Clearly, each of these four axes requires detailed exposition, together with a clear array of the appropriate evidence. This is how there has branched off from each of them subsidiary axes to serve the principal one, clarifying its details and explaining its depths. These four axes mix and interact together in the Qur'ānic symphony in a manner that is precise and concentrated. Then from each of them secondary branches and subsidiary purposes keep arising again and again.

It is important to understand that, apart from the religious sciences that originated specifically because of the need to serve the Qur'ānic text, every other science evolved by the community was also enlisted in its service.

1 A responsible being defined according to legal criteria is an adult who is mentally sound and past the age of puberty.

The influence of the relationship between the Qur'ān and the various sciences on defining the tools and resources of the exegete

THE QUR'ĀN WAS revealed to a community whose particular genius was its exceptionally masterful use of Arabic. At the time of revelation the use of the Arabic language had reached a remarkable degree of aesthetic and semantic perfection. This perfection consisted in the elegant manipulation of words and sentences, together with the capacity to provide intelligent and lucid manners of expression. The Arabs were adept at using and understanding literary expressions. They had an innate talent for discerning and appreciating virtuosity and rejecting mediocrity.

When the Qur'ān was first revealed to them, two things occurred: The first is that they immediately appreciated the greatness, majesty and miraculous quality of its style. Consequently, they recognized that it was clearly beyond human capability and therefore must have a divine origin. Thus, they recognized the truth of it and of its contents of principles, rules, and proofs. The second is that not only were they able to assimilate its form, consisting in its style and structure, but also to comprehend its content, which consists of its meanings and purposes. Thereafter, the Arab nation actively pursued the analysis of its structure and manners of expression. Consequently, a vast network of interrelated sciences was born, the primary purpose and inspiration of which was the need to understand the Qur'ān.

Imām al-Suyūṭī wrote in his *Itqān*[1]:

> Ibn Abī al-Faḍl al-Mursī says in his *Tafsīr*, 'The Qur'ān contains the sciences of the ancients among humans as well as the latecomers, so that in reality its meaning is known only to Him who revealed it, and then to the Messenger of God, save for that which God - Transcendent and Exalted is He - has kept to Himself. Then the majority of the leading Companions inherited this from him, such as the four Caliphs, Ibn Masʿūd, and Ibn ʿAbbās, who was able to say, 'Were I to lose the hobble of a camel, I would be able to find it through the Book of God-Exalted is He.'[2] Then it was inherited by those who followed with excellence; but then resolution faltered, knowledge receded, and scholars became too feeble to carry the burden of its sciences and various arts that the Companions and Followers had carried. Therefore they separated these sciences into distinct specialties, each group concentrating on one specialty. One group concerned itself with linguistics, semantics, counting the letters and investigating their pronunciation, counting the words, verses, *sūras*, *ḥizb*s,

---

1 *Al-Itqān fi ʿUlūm al- Qur'ān* (Expertise in the Sciences of the Qur'ān) is a famous comprehensive reference work on the sciences of the Qur'ān by Imām Jalāl al-Dīn al-Suyūṭī, the great Egyptian scholar and prolific author who died in 911 A.H.

2 The meaning of this statement is that studying the Qur'ān gives the mind a power of penetration conditioned by the principles and rules it contains. The interiorization of these in the mind results in acquiring a Qur'ānic *modus operandi*, which may then be used to solve problems.

nisfs, and *rubʿ*,[3] and number of prostrations, marking the end of each ten verses, counting the number of times a given word is repeated, and the number of similar verses. This was done without delving into its meanings, or meditation on its content. They were called *al-Qurrāʾ*, the Readers or Reciters.

Grammarians concentrated on the grammatical analysis of nouns, verbs and articles. They discussed at length the nouns and their derivatives, and the various kinds of verbs. Some made extensive analyses of ambiguous expressions, while others analyzed it word by word.

Exegetes concentrated on the expressions used, finding that the same word may either mean the same thing every time, or two or more different things. Therefore they left the first as it is, strove to explain what was not obvious, and discussed the probabilities for deciding in favour of one meaning and not another for words with two or more meanings.

Uṣūlīs or principle experts concentrated on the rational proofs, axiomatic principles and deductive arguments, as in His saying (Exalted is He), ***Had there been in them many gods, they would have become corrupted***[4], and

3 A *sūra* is a chapter. There are 114 of these in the Qur'ān .The division into chapters and verses is part of the Revelation, whereas further divisions are artificial ones decided upon by early scholars. The most popular kind of division is that which divides the Qur'ān into thirty equal sections, one to be read every day of the month. A *ḥizb*, also called *juz'*, is thus one thirtieth of the Book, while a *nisf* is half and a *rubʿ* one quarter of a *ḥizb*.

4 Qur'ān, *Sūra al-Anbiyā'*, 22.

other such verses from which they drew their proofs of God's Oneness, affirming His existence, preexistence and subsistence, power and knowledge, and negating anything that is not becoming of Him. They called this science *Uṣūl al-Dīn*, the Science of the Principles of Religion.

Another group studied the meanings of the discourse and saw that some of it was general, some particular. They derived from it the rules for categorizing what is literal and what is figurative, what is specific and what is general, and the manners in which information is conveyed: explicit declarations, synthetic statements, clear as opposed to ambiguous passages, commands and prohibitions, abrogations, and various kinds of analogical reasoning. This science they called *Uṣūl al-Fiqh*, Principles of Jurisprudence.

Yet another group studied what it made licit and what it made illicit, as well as all its other legal rulings. They derived principal rules from which secondary ones branched off and they called this *'Ilm al-Furū'*, the Science of Branches, or *'Ilm al-Fiqh*, the Science of Jurisprudence.

Another group studied the narratives concerned with the ancient past and gone by communities and extracted their stories. They called this *Qaṣaṣ*, History and Narratives.

Others studied the maxims, which are formulations of succinct wisdom, the analogical content, and the sermons that are to shake human hearts and are almost capable of pulverizing mountains. They concentrated on the promises and threats, warnings and good tidings, the mention of death and resurrection, the Mustering and the Judgment, and Heaven and Hell. These were made into sermons and admonitions, and those who delivered them were called orators and preachers.

Others concentrated on the verses regulating inheritance, detailing shares and defining the deserving recipients. This was called *'Ilm al-Farā'iḍ*, the Science of Inheritance. They derived from it the division of shares into halves, thirds, quarters, sixths, and eighths, how to calculate who deserves what, and the rules of testaments.

Others examined the verses pointing out the cosmic marvels in God's creation: the succession of night and day, the movements of the sun and the phases of the moon, and the stars and constellations. From these they came up with *'Ilm al-Mawāqīt*, the Science of Time Keeping.

Writers and poets studied its literary excellence, fluency, harmonious succession of ideas, preambles and conclusions, variations in style, prolixity at certain times and concision at others. From this they derived the science of style and figurative expression.

> The people of subtle indications and inward realities perceived fine meanings to which they gave definitions so as to form a technical vocabulary comprising terms such as extinction and subsistence, presence, fear and awe, intimacy and estrangement, contraction and expansion, and so on.
>
> These are the various arts that the Muslim community derived from the Qur'ān.[5]

This describes only a glimpse of the tremendous intellectual activity exerted by the community to serve the Qur'ānic text and extract from it a large variation of sciences and arts.

This is how the community served the Qur'ānic text and how the various groups of scholars intensively studied the text's brief indications and suggestions, transforming each of them into a working program and a practically applicable method. They so thoroughly researched every subject mentioned in the Qur'ān that out of these studies sciences, arts and crafts were born.

To transform the verses of the Qur'ān into working programs is a most important matter, one with momentous consequences. Only then will the Qur'ān flow through the community and be transformed into practical applications. It is a scientific endeavour that requires much study and research into the very manner of interpreting the Qur'ān.

In brief, the Qur'ān forms the background of all the sources of

5 Suyūṭī, *Itqān*, 2:332.

knowledge of the community, of its sciences, methods of functioning, and cognitive schemes. It defines its identity, shapes its behaviour, and influences its history.

The Qur'ān has bequeathed to the Muslims scientific methods that were tried and tested. These were based upon two firm foundations: Revelation, which is the Qur'ān and the sciences that sprung from it; and field observation confirmed with both research and logical deduction. Thus, the community produced knowledge based on its own sources and methods, its world view, and what followed in the way of historical development and human experience.

The knowledge of the ancestors, the Companions and the Followers, came from inborn aptitudes, for their innate Arab genius allowed them to understand the Qur'ān without recourse to a taught method of analysis. They read the Qur'ān and extracted from it all the above mentioned kinds of knowledge. In subsequent generations this natural aptitude gradually diminished, this impoverishment being compensated for by a gradual development of intellectual methods designed to replace these natural aptitudes with acquired skills consisting of principles, rules and regulations. The innate aptitudes of the first generations of Muslims were analyzed by their successors and, from being intellectual talents innate to the psyche, changed to become documented principles and recorded rules. The successors were then required to study and assimilate them, to be able to match the performance that had once come naturally to their elders. They did this in matters of linguistics, literary performance, and principles. I discussed this in detail in a separate book entitled *al-Ta'ṣīl li-manhaj al-salaf fī'l-fahm,* (Foundations of the Method of Comprehension of the Elders.)

From the fourth century of the *Hijra* onward the community seldom generated new sciences, while doing a great deal to elaborate and refine the sciences already generated and render them more accessible by simplification and summarization.

At the same time other civilizations were actively generating sciences and kinds of knowledge on different bases, using sources of lesser calibre, different philosophies, and different world views. These sciences and methods came to our knowledge at a time when the Muslim community was less than fully healthy and had lost much of its capacity to sift and assimilate new material, so that much confusion was caused, the effects of which we still suffer from today.

The Qur'ān provides a method for assessing such foreign sciences. Since it possesses a philosophy and vision of its own, it imposes upon us the task of reformulating these sciences in a manner suited to our particularities and consistent with our sources and world view.[6] He who strives to find a correspondence between foreign sciences in their current state and the Qur'ān will only increase the present confusion.

The Qur'ān discusses certain kinds of sciences explicitly, others implicitly. It alludes subtly to some, omits others altogether, and forbids yet others for being contrary to its purposes. A detailed analysis of how each science relates to the Qur'ān is therefore

6 Our teacher, Imām ʿAlī Jumʿa, former Grand Muftī of Egypt, has authored a critical study of this important subject of the generation of sciences entitled, "To Generate Sciences is a Duty for Muslims," which is included in his book, *Simāt al-ʿAṣr, Ru'yat muhtamm*; (The Signs of the Age, Vision of a Concerned Person.)

required, for they range from those that are intimately connected with the Qur'ān, to those that bear a non-essential or indirect relation to it, to those that run against its spirit.

One of the best formulations was given by Shaykh Ṭāhir ibn 'Āshūr, an erudite scholar, who said in *al-Taḥrīr wa'l-Tanwīr* (Clarification and Illumination):

> I say: Sciences relate to the Qur'ān in four degrees: The first consists of those sciences which the Qur'ān contains, such as the stories of the Prophets and their communities, discipline of character, jurisprudence and Sacred Law, beliefs, principles, Arabic, and literary performance.
>
> The second consists of sciences that broaden the exegete's knowledge, such as philosophy, astronomy and biology.
>
> The third consists of sciences that are either mentioned in the Qur'ān or whose contents support the contents of the Qur'ān, such as geology, medicine and logic.
>
> The fourth consists of sciences that are unrelated, either because in themselves they are invalid, as for example augury by watching the flight of birds, other divinatory arts, and mythology; or because they are of no practical use in this context, such as the sciences of metres and rhymes.[7]

7 Al-Ṭāhir ibn 'Āshūr, *al-Taḥrīr wa'l-Tanwīr,* 1:45.

I strongly feel that this categorization should be adopted to define the kinds of sciences that an exegete ought to study to qualify for engaging in the exegesis of the Book of God.

The levels of Qur'ānic guidance and their influence on the exegete's understanding of the Qur'ān's universal address

THE SUBJECT OF guidance constitutes one of the most important axes in the Qur'ān. This axis is approached in many different manners; many examples are given to clarify it, and many stories narrated. To understand it we are commanded in the Qur'ān to walk the earth to observe both it and the heavens, the various kinds of creatures, and the higher and lower worlds. It is something to which people are invited both in an explicit and implicit manner. Thus, it constitutes one of the foremost subjects discussed in the Qur'ān.

The theory of guidance in the Qur'ān is based on a general scheme containing many axes, each of which divides into branches, which further divide into commands and prohibitions, maxims and aphorisms, stories and admonishments, and organizational instructions and systems of values.

Guidance in the Qur'ān is of two levels: The first is to guide created beings toward God and motivate them to believe in and obey Him. It is also to grant assistance and success in embracing His Sacred Laws and following His Messengers. This level is pure divine action, shared by no created being. It is called divine guidance and God attributes it to Himself, refusing to allow His creatures any part of it, even the creatures most beloved to Him and those with whom

He is most pleased. He thus denied it to our master Muhammad-may God's blessings and peace be upon him- saying, ***You guide not whom you like, but it is God who guides whom he will, and he knows best those who are guided.***[8]

The second is the guidance of exposition and explanation, of invitation and demonstration, of debate and proof, of providing evidence and arguments and refuting doubts. He who does this does it without possessing any influence upon the hearts or ability to force them to believe him. This is what God commanded His Prophets and Messengers to do, calling it guidance, and attributing it to them. He said about the Prophet, ***You guide indeed to a straight path.***[9] He also attributed it to the followers of the Prophets when He said, ***And from the community of Mūsā are a group who guide by the truth and by it judge with justice.***[10]

This second level of guidance, that of demonstration, is again divided into two kinds: The first is general guidance, whereby God addresses all people indiscriminately, explains the various aspects of the truth to them and elucidates its features to entirely clarify the subject of faith. This discourse does not differentiate between believer and disbeliever, those who accept and those who reject, or those who approve and those who disapprove. Guidance of this kind is a collection of guiding principles and rules that God addresses to all people. From these are derived general laws to govern human society in all its variations. This is the kind of guidance about which God says, ***The month of Ramaḍān in which the Qur'ān was revealed, a guidance for the people and clear signs of guidance and discrimination.***[11]

8 Qur'ān, *Sūra al-Qaṣaṣ*, 56.
9 Qur'ān, *Sūra al-Shūrā*, 52.
10 Qur'ān, *Sūra al-A'rāf*, 159.
11 Qur'ān, *Sūra al-Baqara,* 185.

Here he declares the Qur'ān a guidance for all people, without specifying any particular group or culture.

The second is particular guidance, which consists of the laws, rulings, and divine injunctions that God addresses to those who believe in Him, believe His Messenger, follow His Book, and acknowledge His sovereignty and the supremacy of His sacred law, so that they choose Him for their final recourse. About this kind of guidance God says, ***This is the Book, no doubt in it, a guidance for the God-fearing.***[12] He also says, ***We send down of the Qur'ān that in which there is a cure and a mercy for the believers, but it increases the unjust only in loss.***[13]

It is generally recognized that there is a level of guidance exclusive to God, since it involves creating and bringing into existence, both of which are exclusively divine prerogatives, and another that is carried out by created beings, which is exposition, providing proof, and clarification. However, few are those who have taken notice of the fact that guidance by exposition is itself divided into general and particular, even though the Qur'ān explicitly declares this, for we see God attributing both general and particular guidance to the Qur'ān in a single verse, ***And We send down the Book upon you as a clarification of everything, as well as a guidance, a mercy, and good news for the Muslims.***[14] See how He first makes it a clarification of everything, which here means everything that human beings in general need and is therefore not exclusive to believers, and then goes on to affirm that it is a guidance, a mercy and good news for the Muslims exclusively. Imām ibn Juzay remarked on this in his *al-Tas'hīl li 'Ulūm al-Tanzīl* (Facilitating the Sciences of Revelation), defining "guidance" in this verse as meaning direction, since confined to the God-fearing. Had

12 Qur'ān, *Sūra al-Baqara,* 2.
13 Qur'ān, *Sūra al-Isrā',* 82.
14 Qur'ān, *Sūra al-Naḥl,* 89.

it meant "exposition" it would have involved everyone in general, as in His saying, ***Guidance for mankind.*** This is a clear indication that some guidance is general and thus meant for all people.

Many examples of particular guidance can be found in the verses which begin with, ***O believers!*** There are a little more than eighty of these. The address is to believers, so that the content is exclusively theirs. As for general guidance, it includes all the verses which begin with, ***O humans***, or, ***O Children of Adam!*** These, where the call is addressed to the entire human race, are a little over twenty.

This is why verses starting with ***O believers*** usually carry legal injunctions, whereas those that begin with ***O humans***, or, ***O Children of Adam*** usually carry reminders of principles that are general and concern all humans. Examples of these are the story of how creation began, pointing out and detailing divine blessings and signs, the need to guard oneself against the Devil and his malicious endeavour to turn people away from the signs of God, repeated invitations for them to follow what their Messengers had brought them, the instillation of respect for religion in general, encouraging different communities to get to know each other, and other such common concerns of the human race.

The whole object of general guidance is to promote particular guidance by serving as a preliminary for it. Its goal is to invite all people to a divinely inspired system of values, divine laws and principles of good functioning for human society, then demonstrate how essential, noble and supremely lofty these principles and purposes are, and how they transcend the barriers of time and place, thus serving as evidence of the Qur'ān's divine origin. In this manner they are able to motivate one to accept the religion of God and follow the particular guidance. This is how general guidance prepares one to follow particular guidance.

Here is an example of how this influences the understanding of a Qur'ānic text. God says, ***O humans! We have created you of a male and a female, and made you nations and tribes that you may know each other. The most honourable among you in the sight of God are the most God-fearing. God is Knowledgeable, Aware.***[15] Exegetes have concentrated on the subject of lineages and how boasting about these used to be one of the most reprehensible characteristics of pre-Islamic Arabs. They discussed what the rules of lineages were among them, and as a consequence the question of who is worthy to marry whom, and how Islam lays stress on the fact that God-fearing is more honourable than a noble lineage, and so on. I have read the commentaries on this verse in a number of works such as, among others, *al-Kashshāf, al-Tas'hīl, Mafātīḥ al-Ghayb, al-Muḥarrar al-Wajīz*, al-Qurṭubī, *Rūḥ al-Bayān*, and found them indeed to revolve around these meanings. However, bringing into play the question of general guidance, as explained above, and remembering that the address involves the whole of mankind, brings about the following manner of understanding it. The verse being addressed to all people informs them that they have a common origin. It does this in preparation for an important purpose and noble intent which is shortly to be made clear. It informs them that they were divided into nations and tribes dispersed all over the earth, so that each community had its own unique set of experiences and history. Each had its specific kinds of knowledge, sciences, arts and crafts that over the centuries formed a particular cultural heritage. The sum of each community's experiences, the particular kinds of knowledge it was able to grasp,

15 Qur'ān, *Sūra al-Ḥujurāt,*13.

the sources it depended on, and its ability to use purer sources by relying on revealed knowledge, made each community unique in its qualities. It is obvious that the cultural heritage of the Indians differs from that of the Greeks. Both differ from that of the Persians, which in turn differs from that of the Arabs. Each has a unique nature and identity, and each has its sources of knowledge.

Now there is no doubt that the heritage of every community includes a potential benefit to all human beings, while also including certain deviant particularities, pagan beliefs or national goals that stamp its sciences and arts with a certain character. The Qur'ān points to this in the above verse, and then to the need for mutual acquaintance, which is here said to be the consequence and main purpose of the division of mankind into nations and tribes. Clearly, it is not acquaintance between individuals that is meant, but among whole communities. The result would be the exchange of sciences and experiences, and arts and literature, so that each community would acquaint itself with a heritage that it had not itself produced. This should be followed by sifting and making discriminative choices so that certain things are accepted, others rejected, and some found to require additions or completion.

This happened in our own history when the Mongol waves swamped our lands causing one of the greatest tragedies of our history. Then the ripples of the catastrophe gradually subsided, mutual acquaintance occurred and each community discovered what the other possessed. The Mongols accepted Islam on the one hand, while on the other the Muslims recognized the superiority of the Mongol art of architecture and decoration and adopted much of it, so that it subsists among Muslims as the "Mongol Style" until this day.

The Qur'ān brought a universal invitation addressed to all men for communities to acquaint themselves with each other. This idea could have been adopted by the Muslims, who could have made it the foundation of a global concept called "The Mutual Acquaintance of Civilizations" to replace the concept of the "Clash of Civilizations" which is based on a philosophy that denies God and His Messenger and whose world view is based on conflict. We could have invited others, centuries ago, to a globalization based on our principles, values and identity, which we could have created or played a major part in creating, so that the guidance of the Qur'ān would have reached all people.

The Qur'ān raises the value of God-fearing and makes it the single most important criterion of superiority, which reinforces the value of principles, virtue and good character, and directs people to a noble manner of human interaction motivated in the Muslim by his quest for the good pleasure of God and a high rank in His sight, and in the non-Muslim by his desire for higher values and a noble character. It is sufficient that he may be able to take this from the Qur'ān.

Is it now clear how important it is for the division of guidance into general and particular to be clear in the mind of the exegete, and how important are its consequences.

The Qur'ān Explains Itself

THE FIRST THING the exegete should do is compile similar passages and compare them with each other. It may be that a meaning that is left implicit in one passage is made explicit in another, or that it is stated unconditionally in one place, but accompanied with its conditions in another.

There are profound reasons why the Qur'ān discusses the same subject in several places, and these reasons dictate how far the discussion goes in each instance. Once the exegete gathers them all together, the entire framework becomes clear. The Prophet taught his Companions to do this on several occasions. ʿAbdallāh ibn Masʿūd said, "When it was revealed, ***Those who believe and do not confound their faith with injustice,***[16] the people were distressed and they complained to the Messenger of God, "O Messenger of God, which one of us has not wronged himself?" He answered them, saying, *It is not as you think; have you not heard the words of the virtuous servant,* ***My son, associate none with God, for association is an immense injustice?*** *It is but association* (polytheism and idolatry).[17] Thus was the term injustice used in this sentence in a sense diverging from the usual manner. To grasp this second sense one must be thoroughly familiar with the fundamental

16 Qur'ān, *Sūra al-Anʿām*, 82.
17 The virtuous servant in question is Luqmān, an ancient sage mentioned in *Sūra Luqmān* in the Qur'ān, (31:13).

principles and other comprehensive guidelines of the Sacred Law[18] and its method in defining the things that lead to salvation and those that lead to perdition, so as to understand how the various verses stand in relation to each other. Scholars continued to meditate on this until they came to declare that the whole Qur'ān was as one *sūra*, each part of which sheds light on the rest. Imām Fakhr al-Dīn al-Rāzī says in his *Tafsīr, Mafātīḥ al-Ghayb* (The Keys of the Unseen):

> The Qur'ān is as a single *sūra*, or even a single verse, each part of which confirms and clarifies the rest. Do you not see that the verses containing threats are unconditional, yet they are dependent on the verses of repentance and those of forgiveness?[19]

Shaykh Ṭāhir ibn ʿĀshūr has given important precisions on how to interpret parts of the Qur'ān by means of other parts. He says in *al-Taḥrīr wa'l-Tanwīr*:

> This is not unconditional, for while some parts of the Qur'ān may be interpreted by means of other parts, others are not, since passages which are similar may still carry divergent meanings.[20]

Ibn al-Jawzī has authored a book on the subjects that are mentioned in sum in some passages of the Qur'ān and in detail in others. Ibn

18 Examples of fundamental principles are: "Harm must be removed" and "Doubt does not overrule certainty." As for comprehensive guidelines, they refer to the five major purposes of the Sacred Law which are to preserve life, religion, mind, honour and property.

19 This means that when sinners are threatened with punishment in Hell in one verse and the threat is left unqualified, it is nevertheless conditional because qualified by other verses promising them forgiveness if they repent. *Mafātīḥ al-Ghayb,* 32: 98.

20 *Al-Taḥrīr wa'l-Tanwīr,* 1: 27.

Taymiya draws attention to this in *Uṣūl al-Tafsīr* (Principles of Exegesis), as does Ibn Kathīr at the beginning of his *Tafsīr.* As is well known, he draws on Ibn Taymiya. Suyūṭī does the same in *Al-Itqān*, as did others. This is not far removed from what has become known among latecomers as the "Exegesis of the Qur'ān by Subject", and much has been written about it. One of the best writers on the subject is Shaykh Muḥammad al-Ghazālī who wrote the valuable book, *Naḥw Tafsīr Mawḍū'ī li'l-Qur'ān al-Karīm* (Toward an Exegesis by Subject of the Noble Qur'ān).

The Prophet's *Sunna* is the second of the two Revelations, its source is the Qur'ān and it is the explanation of its meanings

THE PROPHETIC *SUNNA* is the principal explanation of the Qur'ān. Its unique quality is that it is inerrant, so that it is not only the first, but also the most accurate exegesis of the meanings of the Qur'ān. It is infallible and definitive. It complements the Qur'ānic guidance so that both together provide the final legal verdict for any given matter. Imām Suyūṭī says in *al-Itqān*:

> Imām Shāfiʿī said, 'Everything that the community has said is an exegesis of the *Sunna*, and the entire *Sunna* is an exegesis of the Qur'ān.' He also said, 'Every judgment given by the Prophet - may God's blessings and peace be upon him – originates in what he understood of the Qur'ān.' Now I say: this is confirmed by his statement - may God's blessings and peace be upon him, *I make licit for you only that which God has made licit in His Book, and I make illicit only that which God has made illicit in His Book*. This was transmitted thus by Shāfiʿī in *al-Umm*.[21]

Shaykh Ṭāhir al-Jazā'irī said in *Tawjīh al-Naẓar* (Directing Attention):

> A scholar of *Uṣūl* once said, 'What the Prophet said –

21 *Al-Itqān*, 3: 330.

> may God's blessings and peace be upon him – is all in the Qur'ān, either explicitly or in principle, whether the connection is easy or difficult to grasp. He who is capable of understanding will understand, whereas he who is not will not. The same goes for every judgment he passed or verdict he gave. The student's grasp of this matter will be in proportion to the effort he expends and to his capabilities and understanding. Sa'īd ibn Jubayr said, 'No *ḥadīth* was ever transmitted to me in a correct manner from the Messenger of God – may God's blessings and peace be upon him – but that I found confirmation for it in the Book of God.'[22]

This declaration of Sa'īd ibn Jubayr demonstrates an unsurpassable degree of understanding of the meanings of both the Qur'ān and Prophetic *ḥadīths*. When he studies a *ḥadīth* he is able to rise until he reaches the particular fountainhead in the Qur'ān from which springs the *ḥadīth* under study.[23]

A student will be able to grasp more or less of that according to his zeal and effort. Among latecomers the great scholar Ibrāhīm Muḥammad 'Abdallāh al-Khōlī concentrated on this for thirty five years, meditating the Prophetic *ḥadīths* and how they spring from the Qur'ān, to the extent that I have often heard him say, "There is no *ḥadīth* but that I know from which particular verse of the Book of God it springs." He authored on the subject a very enjoyable book entitled *al-Sunna Bayān al-Qur'ān*, (The *Sunna* is the Explanation of

22 *Tawjīh al-Naẓar,* 2: 893.

23 The meaning of this is that a scholar is able to take from the Qur'ān a method of inquiry that leads to the accurate elucidation of the rulings concerning any particular subject.

the Qur'ān), which is in print. I had the privilege of reading that book's concluding chapter in his presence, after which he granted us an *ijāza*[24] for it.

Suyūṭī says in *al-Itqān*:

> Ibn Abī al-Fadl al-Mursī says in his *Tafsīr*, 'The Qur'ān contains the sciences of the first among humans and the last, so that in reality its meaning is known only to Him who revealed it, and then to the Messenger of God, apart from that which God – transcendent and Exalted is He– has kept exclusively to Himself. Then the majority of the leading Companions inherited this from him, such as the four Caliphs, Ibn Mas'ūd, Ibn 'Abbās, who was able to say, 'were I to lose the hobble of a camel, I would be able to find it through the Book of God– Exalted is He.'" Then those who "followed with excellence" inherited it from them; but then resolution faltered, knowledge receded, and scholars became too feeble to continue carrying what the Companions and Followers had carried of its sciences and various arts, so they separated them into distinct specialties and each group took charge of a single specialty.[25]

I say: As is well known, this led to the Muslims generating a brilliant array of techniques to serve the Prophetic utterances. They invented

24 *Ijāza* means permission. An *ijāza* in this context is an authorization from one scholar to another or to a student to use or teach a particular book or subject. There are numerous kinds of *ijāza* ranging from those given to lay people for *baraka* and not implying an effective mastery of the book in question, to high powered ones exchanged among professional scholars.

25 Suyūṭī, *Itqān*, 2:330.

the various sciences of *ḥadīth*, one of the most important of which being the science of the reliability of transmitters. The result was a stupendous scientific achievement unparalleled in any previous community. Scholars who became known as *Ḥāfiẓ* wrote numerous works about the Prophet's clarifications of the Qur'ānic text, thereby producing what became known as *al-Tafsīr bi'l-Ma'thūr*, which means using the Prophetic traditions to shed light on the Qur'ān. One of the most voluminous works of this kind is Imām Suyūṭī's *al-Durr al-Manthūr fi'l-Tafsīr bi'l-Ma'thūr* (Dispersed Pearls: Tradition-Based Exegesis), where he attempted to collect every single tradition that had to do with the Qur'ān from a very wide range of sources. Among the latecomers, the *Muḥaddith* 'Abdallāh Ṣiddīq al-Ghumārī authored a book where he undertook the exegesis of the Qur'ān by means of *ḥadīths*, but was able to finish only as far as *Sūra* Hūd.

The exegete must be acquainted with all the *ḥadīths* and other traditions related to each verse. When the chain of transmission reaching up to the Prophet is uninterrupted, whether effectively or virtually,[26] the text must be accepted as valid. If no such text exists, he must pause and reflect, for each exegete explains the verses according to the state of knowledge of his time, but the Qur'ān is much vaster than the sum of all knowledge possessed by any particular community at any particular time, transcending time, place, and particular conditions. We shall elaborate on that in the coming chapter.

Another benefit that accrues to the exegete from being acquainted with all that has been transmitted to date in relation to a particular

26 Effectively means that the chain of transmission is unbroken and ends with the Prophet himself. Virtually means that the chain of transmission stops with one of the Companions, but the nature of the *ḥadīth* is such that he could not have said it of his own accord, but must have heard it from the Prophet.

subject is the ability to avoid relying exclusively on his own intellectual capacities and make the most of what his predecessors have said, reviewing their thoughts on the subject, in order that they may inspire him with thoughts and opinions which he would perhaps not have reached on his own. The great scholar Abū Bakr al-Rāzī al-Ḥanafī, known as al-Jaṣṣāṣ, remarked as follows in his book, *Aḥkām al-Qur'ān* (Qur'ān Regulations), concerning another exegete, "I know not what has driven him to this. My guess is that it is his lack of knowledge of what previous scholars have said and his exclusive dependence on his own intelligence, without knowledge of what the predecessors have said."[27]

'Abdal-Qādir ibn Badrān discussed in *al-Madkhal* (The Introduction) the opinions that had been emitted by scholars in the past, but were later forgotten. He says:

> They were recorded for another reason, which is to attract attention to the possible range of diversity in the rulings, the variety of intellectual capacities and styles, and that these were the opinions of independent scholars at one time. This is of help in reaching the rank of unconditional or conditional independence. When the latecomers study and compare the work of their predecessors, they will extract instructive benefits; the sum of these may tilt the balance toward a particular opinion. This is important and is the main benefit drawn from recording the opinions of the leading scholars of old.[28]

27 *Aḥkām al-Qur'ān*, 1: 72.
28 *Al-Madkhal,* p. 380.

Studying the Prophetic utterances, besides being a great honour, is one of the most important foundations of exegesis, after which the scholar must study the opinions of other scholars, grasp the gist of them and understand the methods of reasoning, comprehension and deduction by means of which these opinions were reached.

PRINCIPLE FIVE OF QUR'ĀNIC EXEGESIS

The exegete must acquaint himself with the Science of the Principles of Jurisprudence, because it contains important rules for understanding the text and analyzing it

ONE OF THE most important goals for the exegete is to acquaint himself with the tools and methods with which he can analyze the text, break it into components, and understand it. To serve the text by analyzing it and taking it apart, then familiarizing oneself with its components and probing the different meanings of its terms and expressions, leads to comprehension of its aims and purposes and understanding of the rules governing the process of deduction. This is a goal common to both exegetes and scholars of *Uṣūl.* The latter have taken great pains and gone to great lengths in defining these methods and increasing their precision. They started by summing up all the premises derived from the other sciences upon which they depended to reach their goals, making great efforts to penetrate their depths to the maximum by deductive reasoning and blending synthesis, until *'Ilm al-Uṣūl,* the Science of Principles, became fully mature and its methods fully explicit and precise. They went to great lengths to summarize relevant themes from, among others, the sciences of linguistics, grammar and literary expression, making them into separate headings within the Science of Principles. An example is the science that studies the meaning of articles, which is such an important tool for the exegete that Imām Suyūṭī gave it in the *Itqān* the status of a fully fledged science of the Qur'ān. None has studied it more thoroughly or with more precision than the *Uṣūlīs*. Imām al-Subkī said in *al-Ibhāj*:

> The *Uṣūlīs* have researched certain things in the Arabic language that neither the linguists nor the grammarians had ever fathomed before, for the language of the Arabs is quite vast and branches into numerous areas of study. Thus the books of linguistics are concerned with defining expressions according to their obvious meanings, not such subtle meanings as need *Uṣūlī* attention and deeper probing than that of the linguist. For example: "Do!" is a command, while: "Don't!" is a prohibition. "Every" and what resembles it are for generalization; and so on. When you search the books of linguistics you find no satisfaction there, nor mention of what the *Uṣūlīs* have said about it. The same applies to the books of grammar, for they do not contain many of the subtleties that the *Uṣūlīs* have concentrated on and deduced from the language of the Arabs. The latter have come up with arguments and rules of their own that are not included in the art of grammar proper. This and other similar things are what the (Science of the) Principles of Jurisprudence has accomplished.[29]

The work of the exegete, which requires familiarity with the methods of analysis and extraction of content, revolves around analyzing the words of the text, understanding their meanings, and

29 *Al-Ibhāj fī Sharḥ al-Minhāj*, 1: 8.

comprehending what each expression aims at. Thus does the matter return to how the structure and manner of usage of each word indicates its meanings, which is the most profound and precise aspect of *'Ilm al-Uṣūl* or Science of Principles. Imām al-Ghazālī says in his *Mustaṣfā*:

> It is the foundation of the Science of Principles, for the field of the *mujtahid* (independent scholar) is striving to deduce judgments from their principles and pluck them from their branches. For neither do the judgements in themselves depend on the personal choice of the *mujtahid,* nor was the establishment of the four principles that are the Book, *Sunna*, consensus, and intellect, a human choice. The range wherein the *mujtahid* moves and is responsible is his use of his rational powers in extracting judgments and deducing them from their sources, which are the transmitted evidence.[30]

In the light of this, how can anyone dare comment on the Book of God without prior study or thorough training in the Science of Principles?

Ṭāhir ibn 'Āshūr says in *al-Taḥrīr wa'l-Tanwīr*:

> As for the Principles of Jurisprudence, they used not to be considered a tool of exegesis; but as they mentioned commands and prohibitions, and other generalizations which belong to the Principles, only parts were considered suitable tools for exegesis. However, the Principles of Jurisprudence should be considered appropriate tools for exegesis in two respects: First, the

30 *Al-Mustaṣfā*, p. 180.

> Science of Principles contains numerous clarifications concerning the manner in which the Arabs use their language and how that language is derived from its sources, many of which have been overlooked by language experts, an example being implicit meanings which lead to deductions, whether in agreement or disagreement of the original statement.[31]
>
> Al-Ghazālī considers the Science of Principles among the sciences of the Qur'ān and of Qur'ānic rulings, which makes it an obvious tool for exegesis.
>
> Second, the Science of Principles regulates and formulates the rules governing deduction and is therefore the tool of the exegete for the deduction of legal meanings from Qur'ānic verses."[32]

Need we point out that there is even more to it than that? For it should be noted that the student of the art of Principles acquires a complete cognitive methodology that provides him with a set of comprehensive rules governing his inquiries. For instance, he becomes acquainted with the distinction between definitive versus presumptive statements and how this influences understanding; and of the subject of contradiction and preference[33] and how to go about doing it. He also learns the manner in which to identify and extract evidence from the text, and how to use this evidence. All this is clear for whomever assumes the task of clarifying what is meant by the words of God.

---

31 An example of implicit meaning is the Qur'ānic command not to speak rudely to one's parents. Jurisprudents deduce from this that it would obviously be much more reprehensible to beat them. Similarly they deduce that it would be praiseworthy to speak gently to them and serve them.

32 *Al-Taḥrīr wa'l-Tanwīr*, 1: 26.

33 When texts contradict each other scholars have recourse to a sophisticated methodology for deciding which meaning should be given precedence over the other.

The need of the exegete to keep up with the amplifications in the meanings of verbal expressions that accompany the expansion of the limits of knowledge of a given civilization and the cumulative effects of its experiences

SCHOLARS OF PRINCIPLES say, "Using language is the attribute of the speaker, while inferring meaning is the attribute of the listener; and the convention precedes both."[34] This means that it is the role of the recipient or listener to understand the meaning of speech according to the known conventions of the language. It also means that the listener receives speech and analyzes it, extracting the meaning and trying to fathom it to reach the purpose of the speaker. All this is governed by the conventions of the language that dictate the manner in which it is used, thus creating a common field between the speaker and the listener that allows the exchange of meanings. It is on the basis of this exchange that human society progresses and knowledge accumulates and is circulated among the people, so that civilization flourishes.

This convention-governed process depends on relating every word to the meaning or meanings for which it was created ever since the very first appearance and stabilization of the language, so that it is no longer possible to alter this meaning or substitute another for it,

34 Ibn Juzay, *Taqrīb al-Wuṣūl*, p. 55.

while leaving an adequate margin of variation, governed by precise rules, to allow the necessary range of meanings, whether partial or complementary, to be derived from the original meaning of the word. There must be a connection between the various meanings of the same word, so that with reflection one may pass from the original to the newly found meaning, and there must be widespread acceptance of these new meanings so that there is a consensual acceptance of them, and the process of understanding and communicating this understanding is kept up. Failing these conditions, there will be divergent conceptions of the meanings of words, these meanings will lose their capacity of being communicated, and there will result such extreme difficulty in exchanging ideas that it may lead to a collapse of human society.

Reference to linguistic criteria in order to understand applies to single words. Sentences, however, require in addition that account be taken of the relations between their various components. Understanding these components depends on factors other than linguistics, such as the power of imagination of the listener, his awareness of the various possibilities of the composition, or prior knowledge of the intentions of the speaker, so that upon hearing certain expressions his understanding is already broad enough to grasp them. On the other hand, for him who has no such knowledge, understanding will stop at the obvious meaning, without any possibility of extending it. Clearly, the speaker must have understood these meanings so as to be able to include them in his manner of expression, before leaving the task of taking notice and apprehending them to the alertness of the listener and the prior presence of such meanings in his mind.

Thus can each listener's capacity for understanding extend to include wider meanings in proportion to the extent of his knowledge and background information.

Most human beings, however, approximate each other in knowledge and are governed by the givens of their time. They are not able to conceive of things which time will reveal only after they are gone, and are therefore obviously incapable of talking about them. A man of genius who can predict some future things in one way or another will speak of them, and then if his predictions are confirmed by events, he will be considered an extraordinary phenomenon that deserves close study. Such for instance are the well-known predictions of Nostradamus.

Compared with these limitations, how should we conceive of the comprehensive all-embracing divine knowledge from which nothing is hidden? God decides what happens and when, and what new sciences and information are to be discovered. Then He includes in His speech certain indications to that effect, so that whenever something new supervenes, there are references to it already to be found in the text. For the text of the Qur'ān, its every word and expression, is from God. Therefore it is never contradicted by an enlargement in the limits of knowledge at any particular time. This quality is clearly beyond human powers. The ability of human beings to predict the future or imagine what new things it may bring is quite restricted, which is why whenever in the past human whims led to tampering with Scripture, the result was to impose certain limits on the text which were eventually proved false. This is why God has promised to protect and preserve the integrity of the Qur'ān, while other Scriptures, altered by human hands, are in conflict with reality. It is well known how this had led at one time to the problem of religion versus science in Europe. This was discussed by Maurice Bucaille in his widely read book, *The Bible, the Qur'ān, and Science.*[35]

Thus it is that the more human knowledge increases and new sciences and discoveries occur, they find that unlike human declarations, the Qur'ānic text remains in perfect accord with these. The more the person who reads the Qur'ān becomes acquainted with various other sciences and philosophies, the broader the scope of the Qur'ānic text becomes for him. For as Muṣṭafā Ṣādiq al-Rāfiʿī says in *Tārīkh Ādāb al-ʿArab* (History of Arab Literature), "The Qur'ān is a verbal presence that is designed to perpetually remain with mankind."[36] This is why the Qur'ān has retained its freshness across the centuries, so that its wonders have never been exhausted, nor has its source ever run dry. On the contrary, it becomes ever more bountiful the more humanity increases in knowledge and civilization.

Ṭāhir ibn ʿĀshūr says in *al-Taḥrīr wa'l-Tanwīr*:

> The second kind of scientific matchlessness is divided into two sections, one where it suffices to hear and understand, and another which needs acquaintance with the foundations of various sciences to grasp its miraculousness, so that it gradually becomes clearer just as the day gradually becomes clearer at dawn, according to the limits of understanding and the development of the various sciences.[37]

Had any human being been capable of expressing himself on any given subject in a manner, as described above, immune from ever being contradicted with the expansion of the limits of knowledge

35 Maurice Bucaille, *The Bible, the Qur'ān, and Science*, translated from the French, 3rd edition., Editions Seghers, Paris.
36 *Tārīkh Ādāb al-ʿArab*, 1: 14.
37 *Al-Taḥrīr wa'l-Tanwīr*, 1: 127.

with time, his words would have been considered miraculous. The Qur'ān not only achieves this, but also achieves many other major goals, the most obvious of which is that it provides a miraculous Sacred Law. In addition, it contains the knowledge of all-embracing principles, noble legal aims, information about unknown things, past and future, the principles of beliefs, the definition of the principal virtues, refuting the deviant sects and irrational currents of thought that have appeared throughout human history, shaping the human soul with its emotions and reactions, drawing attention to the essentials of human society and the causes of corruption and deviancy, and offering practical advice for guidance and virtue. It also directs attention to the hereafter and the momentous events that are to happen there, and the fate of human beings, judgment, reward in heaven, or punishment in hell. This is no less than miraculous many times over.

The exegete must be familiar with all these kinds of knowledge and with every kind of science, and with their principles, so that his meditations on the Qur'ān become as broad as possible and he can see how the Qur'ān is truly a guidance for all beings.

The effects of grasping the various manners in which the Qur'ān affects the soul on understanding and analyzing the text, and the necessity of learning that method

THIS IS A principle to which the exegete should devote concentrated attention, even though it escapes the awareness of most other people. For the exegete, being the one who studies the purposes and aims of the Qur'ān, needs to acquaint himself with the various manners in which it is able to move souls, how it motivates them into activity, causes them to exert effort, and gives them zeal to achieve its purposes, or arouses anxiety and dread of falling into what it forbids. These the exegete must comprehend and feel, and explore their depths and how they penetrate the subconscious. He must also grasp how Qur'ānic words and expressions inspire feelings of yearning or fear, encouragement or discouragement, magnification or contempt, and so on. The exegete must grasp these indications, understand their purposes, bring them into the limelight, then magnify them until he makes them rise to the conscious level. At this point his reader will have understood and will respond with yearning or fear in a manner so deep that it may change his life. At this point, it will be possible for people to understand such deep purposes and subtle secrets of the Qur'ān. An example is the secret behind leaving the term "life" in the indefinite in the verse, ***You shall indeed find them most anxious***

for life, and of those who associate,[38] as well as in the following verse, ***There is life for you in retaliation, men possessed of minds, that you may fear.***[39] This is abundant in the Book of God.

This principle depends on two axes. The first consists of the science of literary expression which is concerned with the intricacies of the language, the shifts in meaning and the possibilities thus created by every change or alteration in the composition or derivation of words and expressions. The second is psychology, which is concerned with studying the human soul, why and how it acts, and how it responds to various stimuli. Major advances towards discovering the secrets of the human soul have been made in this area. Many schools and methods have appeared, branching into numerous specialties, where the subject is studied according to the paradigms of a materialistic experimental science that attempts to fathom the depths of the soul solely through experiment. This science became well established and received widespread acceptance in the absence of our own Islamic research methods based on an understanding of the nature of the soul and its transformations according to our two well established sources of knowledge: Revelation – since the Qur'ān contains a complete description of the human soul – and observation.

The Qur'ān teaches a lofty divine method in the practical application of this knowledge, in clarifying its purposes, and in choosing its words and verses to influence the soul. When the exegete becomes familiar with this method and its details, he is able to perceive within each word, expression, or sentence the effect it is intended to produce on the soul.

Imām al-Khaṭṭābī says in *Bayān I'jāz al-Qur'ān*, (Demonstration of

38 Qur'ān, *Sūra al-Baqara*, 96.
39 Qur'ān, *Sūra al-Baqara*, 179.

the Matchlessness of the Qur'ān):

> The matchlessness of the Qur'ān has another aspect that most people are unaware of, so much so that only rare individuals are aware of it, which is its effect on the hearts and influence on the soul. There is no poetry or prose, other than the Qur'ān, which when heard arouses in the heart such sweetness and pleasure at times and awe and fear at others. It is able to bring joy and optimism into the heart and expand the breast; and then it changes into fear, dread, apprehension, and terror. It causes the skins to shiver and the hearts to panic, and penetrates between the souls and their innermost thoughts and firmest beliefs.[40]

Imām Abū Bakr al-Bāqillānī had much to say about this in *I'jāz al-Qur'ān* (The Matchlessness of the Qur'ān), pointing out the effect the light of the Qur'ān most evidently has upon the heart and mind. He describes how:

...it suffuses the senses, flows through the veins, and fills one with certainty and insight. He then describes how "terror comes over one from one side, even while he is swayed by delight from another, then entirely soothed from yet another."He asks whether you can see how "the ignorant fall down under the feet of heedlessness, where they plummet under the shadows of indigence and abasement? Do you see their worth with the eye it should be seen with, their degrees where they should be seen?"He goes on describing the effects of the Qur'ān on the heart in a most powerfully poetic style, then adds that its central importance is rendered evident by the fact

40 *Bayān I'jāz al-Qur'ān*, p. 70.

> "it was made the basis of the ritual prayer, which ranks only after faith itself in importance, and second only to *Tawḥīd* in necessity; that to memorize it was made incumbent, and that the young and the old are enjoined to recite it. Furthermore, as is decreed in His words, ***And when you recite the Qur'ān seek protection in God from the repudiate devil,***[41] it should be magnified even before its recitation is begun. There is no order to seek protection before initiating any act save reciting the Qur'ān. Does not that indicate to you how great its rank is, how heavy in the scales and lofty in position it is?[42]

I say: a number of serious attempts were made to explore the secrets of the Qur'ān in dealing with the human soul, among which *al-Qur'ān wa 'Ilm al-Nafs* by Dr. Muḥammad 'Uthmān Najātī, and *al-Ta'bīr al-Qur'ānī wa'l-Dalāla al-Nafsiya* of Dr.'Abdallāh Muḥammad al-Juyūsī.

Certain Qur'ān scholars may take a hostile stance toward this, finding it strange that we should wish to make psychology intrude upon the well established traditional Qur'ānic sciences. To this I say that the Muslim community has extracted, over the centuries, entire complex systems of rules for interrelated domains of knowledge and devised for them suitable methods of applications, in order to serve the Qur'ān. This is how the sciences of the Arabic language and of principles, among others, developed. This intellectual movement to serve the Qur'ān should continue so that whatever new developments occur in matters of knowledge or methodology should be utilized

41 Qur'ān, *Sūra al-Naḥl,* 98.
42 *I'jāz al-Qur'ān,* p. 202.

in Qur'ānic studies. It is incumbent upon the community to study, assimilate, summarize and sift these before making them tools to serve the Qur'ān; otherwise the Muslims will become cut off from the flow of blessings of the Qur'ān and become veiled from it.

The stories of the Prophets are expositions of the various cognitive styles governing mankind throughout history

STORIES OF THE Prophets were recounted in the Qur'ān for numerous divine purposes, one of which was to strengthen the Prophet's heart, then the hearts of his heirs, those who would carry to the people after him the heritage of prophethood and the lights of guidance. These are the scholars, guides, and summoners to God in full awareness, as the Real says, ***And all that we narrate to you of the news of the Envoys is to strengthen your heart.***[43] Another purpose is that they are food for thought and meditation for the intellectually minded, for He says – Transcendent is He, ***in their stories are lessons for those endowed with focused minds.***[44] His saying, ***lessons for those endowed with focused minds,*** indicates that these stories need extensive scrutiny to allow those with such minds to extract all their major benefits. Ṭāhir ibn 'Āshūr has discussed at great lengths in the seventh introduction of *al-Taḥrīr wa'l-Tanwīr* the benefits – of which he mentioned ten – gained from these stories, together with explanations of how the Qur'ān uses them to achieve certain goals.

I have meditated on the stories of the Prophets in the Qur'ān and an all-inclusive meaning appeared to me which makes the benefit

43 Qur'ān, *Sūra Hūd,* 120.
44 Qur'ān, *Sūra Yūsuf,* 111

from them far greater than if derived from a simple historical narration, which does not imply a denial of the importance of such narrations. This is because each of these stories describes a particular style of deviancy, then analyzes and refutes it. Each thus constitutes an occasion for discussing one of the major questions that have always preoccupied human thought, and for correcting the errors in one particular philosophy. To demonstrate that the stories of the Prophets in the Qur'ān contain discussions of the essentials of the various deviant patterns of thought that have kept repeating themselves throughout history, let us point out that there were various versions of secularism throughout history, for the idea of separating worldly from religious affairs is not new, neither is it a product of the European Renaissance. It is an ancient pattern, an example of which is given in the Qur'ān in the story of the people of Shu'ayb – may peace be upon him – who are reported to have said, ***O Shu'ayb, does your prayer command you that we should abandon what our fathers have worshipped, or that we dispose of our wealth as we wish? You have always been an*** [eminently] ***intelligent and wise man.***[45] In addition to their disbelief, the people of Shu'ayb had another problem, which was that they recognized no connection between piety, prayer, and virtue on the one hand and their financial affairs on the other, believing that there was no relation between religious and economic affairs. This is why they found it strange that he thought there should be one. Thus does the story of Shu'ayb contain a Qur'ānic discussion of the question of secularism and a refutation of its arguments. It makes clear its harm and suggests the alternative, namely the divine teachings concerning the subject.

We can thus understand why God chose those particular stories from

45 Qur'ān, *Sūra Hūd,* 87.

a large number of other possibilities, which can be understood from His saying – Exalted is He, ***We have sent Envoys before you, some We have narrated to you and some We have not.***[46] The few stories chosen are those that, being suitable as occasions to discuss major human concerns and main philosophical ideas, are sufficient and obviate the need to narrate the stories of the many other divine envoys.

The exegete must therefore approach the story of Shuʿayb – may peace be upon him – by gathering together all the passages that mention it, studying the divine manner of handling the question of secularism, how God taught Shuʿayb the precise manner in which to refute it, and the particular arguments that the Qur'an chooses to use. To know what he should be looking for in the Qur'an in the way of argumentation, the exegete should also acquaint himself thoroughly with the history of secularism, how it developed, and its various forms. An example would be the manner Dr. ʿAbdal-Wahhāb al-Masīrī discusses these questions in his book, *al-ʿIlmāniyya al-Juz'iyya wa'l- ʿIlmāniyya al-Shāmila* (Partial and Total Secularism).

Recognizing that there is more to the stories of the Prophets than the immediate lessons in wisdom they convey, the strengthening of the heart they produce, and the setting of behavioural examples to be followed, but are also discussions of the main trends of human thought over the centuries, will push the limits of what can be found there so that new Qur'ānic studies can develop to be used in refuting contrary philosophical trends of thought, both old and modern.

The story of Mūsā – may peace be upon him – when his people asked him to see God openly, is an important Qur'ānic discussion of the experimental method which confines knowledge to the limits of

46 Qur'ān, *Sūra Ghāfir,* 87.

sensory perception.

As for the story of Lūṭ – may peace be upon him – it discusses the question of homosexuality, while that of Hūd – may peace be upon him – discusses the question of military dictatorships and the dreams of hegemony and illusory empire-making which have moved so many nations over the centuries.

The gist of this is that the stories of the noble Prophets – may God's peace be upon them – contain universal lessons of much broader relevance than the immediate context. These universal lessons result from the analysis and discussion of the main deviant patterns of thought that have plagued humanity since the dawn of time, clothing themselves in a variety of forms and colours according to the givens of each particular civilization.

This subject needs to be studied, analyzed, and detailed to bring to light the particular manner in which the Qur'ān responds to each of these, how it discusses and refutes them. May God assist us in undertaking a number of studies to fully investigate this.

The axes of the various *sūras* of the Qur'ān and their influence on understanding the text

EACH *SŪRA* (CHAPTER) of the Qur'ān has a well-defined axis[47] upon which it is built, around which it revolves, and which it explains and expounds with examples, detailed images, and stories. These are followed by legal injunctions, instructions for character reform, and discussions of ideas. These components form an interrelated tissue of partial purposes which, by interacting and enriching each other, in the end confirm and clarify the main axis around which the *sūra* revolves. Each *sūra* is thus composed of a number of purposes. Each purpose springs from the single source that is that of the main axis, constituting a particular aspect of it, so that the structure of the *sūra* is built on discussing and explaining each of these purposes in turn. As these are clarified, the full contour of the main axis becomes apparent. It is necessary for these to be arrayed in the Qur'ānic text in a manner that is harmonious and brings out the connections between them, however subtle. Moreover, when a particular point is discussed and comes near to being completely elucidated, tidings appear of the next point in line, and so on until the main purpose of the *sūra* is fulfilled.

To understand what an axis is, let us take as an example the *Fātiḥa*,

47 The axis is the fountainhead from which spring the succession of ideas in a *sūra*, as well as the various manners in which these ideas interrelate.

the first *sūra* of the Qur'ān and the first thing a human being hears of the words of God. We find that, since the *sūra* revolves around the relationship between the Creator and the created, namely worship from the created and assistance from the Creator, the main axis is, ***You it is that we worship and You it is that we ask for help***.

As for *Sūra al-Baqara*, which is the first to follow upon the *Fātiḥa*, its axis is His saying, ***When his Lord said to him, "Surrender!" He said, "I surrender to the Lord of all beings."***[48] The *sūra* revolves around the question of surrendering to God and how it is the greatest portal of entry into the state of realizing one's slavehood to God and receiving His assistance, as stated in the previous *sūra*, the *Fātiḥa*. The foundation is complete surrender to God's might and lordship, to His being the sole sovereign, alone worthy of worship and sole source of the Sacred Law.

When this concept becomes firmly grasped by the mind and soundly established in the heart, the Muslim can then be moved to the next stage, which is the concept of election[49] around which revolves the next *sūra*, that of *Āl-'Imrān*. The axis of this *sūra* is a single verse stating that, ***God has chosen Ādam, Nūḥ, the family of Ibrāhīm and the family of 'Imrān over all beings; the seed of each other. God is He who hears and knows.***[50]When the question of election is made clear and God's choice is surrendered to Him, we are moved to a particular kind of election. The election in question consists of the differences in character between people and the different attributes of each sex, upon both of which legal rulings are based. At this point the *sūra* that follows upon *Āl-'Imrān, Sūra al-Nisā'* intervenes to discuss the

48 Qur'ān, *Sūra al-Baqara*, 131.
49 Election in this context refers to the reality that God bestows certain characteristics or attributes upon certain people of His choice to make them superior to others, as in the case of divine Envoys, or merely different, as in the case of males and females.
50 Qur'ān, *Sūra Āl-'Imrān,* 33, 34.

question of recognizing the specific attributes of each sex, before assigning to each the rights and duties specifically consonant with these attributes. Upon this base rests the stability and durability of human societies. The axis of this *sūra* is the following verse, ***Desire not that by which God has favoured one of you over the other. To the men a share of what they earn and to the women a share of what they earn; and ask God of His favour. Surely God knows everything.***[51]

It should now be apparent that each *sūra* of the Qur'ān deals with a particular major issue, starting with the question of slavehood to God in the *Fātiḥa*, that of surrender in *al-Baqara*, of election in *Āl-'Imrān*, of the recognition of divergence and preservation of rights in *al-Nisā'*, and of the preservation of bonds in *al-Mā'ida*. We can discern about one hundred such issues which together constitute the essentials of revealed religion, the most important ideas and concepts that religion addresses in its definition of the relationship between the Creator and the created.

Once the exegete recognizes the axis of each *sūra*, he is able to use its verses and passages in that context, and there shall appear to him new meanings in the composition and structure of each *sūra,* and he will understand how different passages relate to each other.

Scholars may disagree on which verse constitutes the axis of a particular *sūra* or even on the very issue that constitutes the axis of that *sūra*. There may be elaborate debates about the difference between what constitutes an axis and what a purpose. These differences will surely enrich Qur'ānic studies and lead to uncovering dimensions of meaning that had gone unnoticed before, for this approach is new and I have seen no previous authors mentioning it. I have devoted a

51 Qur'ān, *Sūra, al-Nisā'*, 32.

whole volume entitled, *al-Imʿān fī Maḥāwir Suwar al-Qur'ān* (An in-Depth Study of the Axes of the Qur'ān), which I ask God to allow me to complete. I have also recently come upon a book entitled, *Naẓrat'al-ʿAjlān fī Aghrāḍ al-Qur'ān* (A Quick Glance at the Purposes of the Qur'ān), by Muḥammad ibn Kamāl Aḥmad al-Khaṭīb, printed many years ago by al-Maṭbaʿa al-ʿAṣriyya in Damascus and introduced by the great scholar Muṣṭafā al-Zarqā. The author speaks of each *sūra* as having a single subject and how there is consequent order in the succession and interrelatedness of the subject it discusses. Shaykh Muṣṭafā al-Zarqā explicitly remarks that this is a new approach, never before attempted in the same manner. This book is indeed useful and not far removed from what we are about. Despite not clarifying the meanings in the manner described above, it is nevertheless a step on the way.

Fundamental principles of the Qur'ān or independent inference[52]: a practical method applied by the community over the centuries to derive benefit from the verses of the Qur'ān

SCHOLARS HAVE PERSISTENTLY striven to understand Qur'ānic expressions, inventing as they went along the necessary tools and methods that would allow them to extract the maximum possible benefits from every word, expression or passage. Understanding a sentence became a meticulous endeavour to be achieved in several stages. First one must define the meanings of every single word. Then one must proceed to explore the possible variations resulting from the particular composition of the sentence. Following this the most appropriate of possible meanings must be chosen according to the context, as well as according to factors in the composition of the sentence itself, such as which expression precedes which, or which comes at the conclusion of the sentence. The subject of context thus became an important governing principle to understand the Qur'ānic text. Shāh Waliyyullāh al-Dihlawī said in *al-Fawz al-Kabīr* (The Great Success):

> To be fair the exegete should study the explanation of

52 Fundamental principles are the major concepts in matters of beliefs and legislation regulating both civilization and acts of worship. The principles in question here, however, are only those derived from independent inference, which means understanding the meaning of a particular sentence independently from the context.

> every unusual expression in two ways, weighing it in all objectivity twice: once according to the conventional use of the Arabs, which will give him indications as to which meaning is more appropriate and more likely to be intended, and a second according to what precedes and succeeds the expression in question. This he should do after he has mastered the premises of this science, searched for the various uses of the same term in different contexts, and studied the possible consequences of ascribing a particular meaning to a term, until he comes to understand which meanings are more likely to have been intended.[53]

When we examine how the elders of this community and the succeeding generations of scholars have dealt with this question in the course of history, we find that they evolved a unique and admirable practical method to extract the benefits of Qur'ānic sentences. This they did by first studying the immediate meaning dictated by the context, then the other possible meanings which, while nevertheless retaining their qualities of being divine, sacred, and authoritative, are independent of the context. These latter meanings they separated from the context and took as independent sentences sufficient unto themselves. This manner of approaching the text is actually older than these efforts, for it is reported to have been done by the Prophet himself – may God's blessings and peace be upon him.

Ṭāhir ibn 'Āshūr says in *al-Taḥrīr wa'l-Tanwīr*:

> Evidence for this position of ours is found in that which we have received in the way of recorded and transmitted

53 *Al-Fawz al-Kabīr*, p. 181.

explanations of certain verses of the Qur'ān by the Prophet – may God's blessings and peace be upon him – some of which are undoubtedly not the immediate primary meanings of the verses. With reflection it becomes clear that the Prophet – may God's blessings and peace be upon him – wished to rouse the minds with his explanations to strive to extract the furthermost meanings of the text. An example is that reported by Abū Saʿīd ibn al-Muʿallā who said, "The Messenger of God called me while I was praying, so I did not answer him. Once I was finished and came to him, he said, 'What kept you from answering me?' I said, 'O Messenger of God, I was praying.' He said, 'Does not God the Exalted say, ***O believers, respond to God and the Messenger when he summons you?***'"[54] There is no doubt that the primary meaning of responding here is obeying, as in His saying – Exalted is He – in another passage, ***Those who responded to God and the Messenger after they were stricken with injury.***[55] The primary meaning of the "summons" is guidance; witness His saying, ***They summon to good.***[56] In the first verse the verb ***summons*** is related to the rest of the verse which is His saying, ***to that which will give you life.*** Meaning: That which will be profitable to you in an essential manner. However, the Prophet – may God's blessings and peace be upon him – disregarding the context, used the term ***respond*** to mean answer when being called.

54 Qur'ān, *Sūra Āl-ʿImrān,* 24.
55 Qur'ān, *Sūra Āl-ʿImrān,*172.
56 Qur'ān, *Sūra Āl-ʿImrān,* 104.

Similarly, his saying – may God's blessings and peace be upon him, *People are gathered on Resurrection Day barefoot, naked, and uncircumcised;* ***As We began the first creation We shall repeat it.***[57] The verse quoted in this *ḥadīth* compares the second creation, which is the resurrection, to the first, in order to refute those who deny the possibility of resurrection, just as in His saying, ***Were We exhausted by the first creation? No, but they are in confusion concerning the new creation.***[58] And His saying, ***He it is who begins creation then repeats it, and it is so easy for Him.*** [59] This then is the ground for similarity. However, since it is possible for similarity to be pushed further, the Prophet informed us that that is also required, so that the similarity with the first creation will also include being naked and barefoot.

Another example is His saying, ***Should you ask forgiveness for them seventy times, God would still not forgive them.***[60] When 'Umar ibn al-Khaṭṭāb asked the Prophet not to pray the Funeral Prayer on 'Abdallāh ibn Ubay ibn Salūl[61], since God had forbidden him to ask forgiveness for them, the Prophet answered him, *My Lord has left the choice to me and I shall ask more than seventy times.* Here he says that he is given a choice, despite the fact that the immediate meaning is that it will make no difference to them whether he does or not. Furthermore, he took the number seventy literally despite the fact that the context indicates that it merely serves to indicate a large number. His choice was obviously that since the literal meaning was there for the taking, he would take it.

---

57 Qur'ān, *Sūra al Anbiyā'*, 104.
58 Qur'ān, *Sūra Qāf,* 15.
59 Qur'ān, *Sūra al-Rūm,* 27.
60 Qur'ān, *Sūra al-Tawba,* 80.
61 'Abdallāh ibn Ubay ibn Salūl was the chief of the hypocrites, a faction of people from Madina who pretended outwardly to be Muslims, while harbouring enmity in their hearts and plotting to overthrow Islam.

Again when Umm Khālid bint al-Aswad[62] came to Madina, the Prophet recited, ***He brings the living out of the dead,***[63] using the verse in a metaphorical manner different from the immediate meaning.

It also seems that the prostrations during Qur'ān recitation[64], assuming they are expressions of the Prophet's understanding and application of the text, are governed by this principle. On the other hand, if they are revealed orders, it would be even more to the point, since this would indicate that God encourages various meanings to be extracted from the text so long as they do not contradict its purposes.

Similar things have been reported from the Companions and the leading scholars who succeeded them. An example is the episode where 'Amr ibn al-'Āṣ woke up one cold morning, in the course of a campaign, having incurred major impurity during the night. He performed *tayammum*[65], saying, "God says, ***Kill not yourselves, God is merciful indeed to you.***[66] The immediate meaning of the verse, however, is a prohibition of murder and bloodshed.

Yet another example was when Iraq was conquered under 'Umar and the victorious army requested him to divide the land between them. He said, "If I divide it among you, those Muslims who are later to come from the conquered territories will find nothing similar to

62 This lady's father was a pagan, thus spiritually dead, while she was a believer and a Companion of the Prophet, thus very much alive.

63 Qur'ān, *Sūra al-An'ām,* 95.

64 When there is mention of a ritual prostration in the course of a Qur'ān recitation, the Prophet's instructions are to stop the recitation, prostrate one's forehead to the ground, then raise it and resume the recitation. Most scholars are of the opinion that there are fourteen such verses in the Qur'ān.

65 Ritual purification with dust in the absence of water.

66 Qur'ān, *Sūra al Nisā'*, 29.

what you found. I think we should make it public property, the revenue of which to be divided among all the Muslims of this land every season. God says, ***And those who came after them.***"[67] The verse refers to the spoils taken from the Jewish tribes of Qurayẓa and al-Naḏīr, whereas, "those who came after them" are the Muslims who accepted Islam after the victory mentioned earlier in the text.

There is also the manner in which 'Umar chose to begin the Muslim calendar with the day the Prophet emigrated, basing himself on the verse that says, ***A mosque founded, from the first day, on God-fearing is more worthy of you to stand in.***[68] The immediate meaning is that the mosque was founded by God-fearing men. The expression allows a variant understanding that it was founded on the first day, which is the day most worthy of being named the first day of Islam. The firstness here becomes relative.

The *Fuqahā'* (Jurisprudents) have taken as evidence for the legality of *Ja'āla* and *Kafāla*[69] His saying in the story of Yūsuf – may peace be upon him, ***He who brings it shall receive a camel's load; and that I guarantee,***[70] as we said in the third introduction, although this is the story of something long gone, in an extinct community, and there is neither approval nor disapproval in the text. It is not part of a revealed law, but [they adduced it] simply because the Qur'ān, having mentioned it, did not disapprove.

---

67 Qur'ān, *Sūra al-Hashr,* 10.
68 Qur'ān, *Sūra al-Tawba,* 108.
69 *Ja'āla* is to say: "If anyone brings me back my lost camel I shall give him so much money." This is considered a valid binding contract and it becomes the right of he who bring back the camel to receive the stated sum. As for *Kafāla*, it is to become a guarantor for someone else, usually in cases of loans and debt settlements.
70 Qur'ān, *Sūra Yūsuf,* 72.

Another thing of the same kind is al-Shāfiʿī using as proof for the authoritative status of consensus (*Ijmāʿ*) and the illegality of contravening it, His saying – Exalted is He, ***He who opposes the Messenger after the guidance has become clear to him, and follows other than the path of the believers, We shall turn him over to what he has turned to and We shall roast him in Hell, an evil destiny.***[71] The context is one of addressing the idolaters. The immediate meaning thus indicates one particular kind of opposition and of following other than the path of the believers. Nevertheless, al-Shāfiʿī deduced from it the authoritative status of consensus, considering it part of the complete meaning of the verse.[72]

Our Shaykh ʿAbdal-Ghafūr Muṣṭafā Jaʿfar says in his book, *Buḥūth fī ʿUlūm al-Qur'ān al-Karīm* (Studies in the Sciences of the Noble Qur'ān):

> This issue – that of taking every possible meaning, asserting that they are all intended – is, according to divergent schools, acceptable rationally, linguistically, as literary expression, and legally. Exegetes have practiced it. I cannot number the evidence I have collected to prove it; he who wishes to will be able to discern them easily. The evidence comes from transmitted *tafsīr*, which is the *tafsīr* of the Companions – may God be pleased with them all, that of the Followers, then the vastly abundant work of scholars from all schools. All these prove the case and confirm it, so that we know that to confirm divergent meanings,

71 Qur'ān, *Sūra al- Nisā'*, 115.
72 *Al-Taḥrīr wa'l-Tanwīr.*

> whether they are equal or some are more probable than others, is an opinion that is acceptable.[73]

This is where the issue known as the "Independent Inferences from the Qur'ān" comes to the fore. Despite being practiced and applied by generations of scholars, producing numerous scientific axes, all having their origin in the Qur'ān, its rules have yet to be explicitly described and its methodology discussed, as well as the precise manner in which it should be utilised in a systematic manner.

The first to study the phenomenon of Qur'ānic fundamental principles according to our Shaykh, the Grand Muftī of Egypt, 'Alī Jum'a, was Dr. Muḥammad al-Sayyid Badr, late head of the department of the Philosophy and History of Law at the Faculty of Law at the University of 'Ayn Shams, in a book he entitled, *al-Mabādi' al-'Āmma fi'l-Qur'ān al-Karīm*, (General Principles in the Noble Qur'ān).[74]

Shaykh 'Alī Jum'a wrote a most important article that was published in *al-Mawsū'a al-Qur'āniyya al-Mutakhassissa* (Professional Qur'ānic Encyclopaedia)[75], published by the Supreme Committee of Islamic Affairs, where he set firm foundations for the concept of Qur'ānic principles. He provides a definition for it, explains its properties, shows the difference between it and between those realities that must be taken by faith, as well as those derived from observation, then between it and between legal rulings and the rules governing both Jurisprudence and the Principles of Jurisprudence. He then gives a few principles as examples, explains them, then says:

> The Qur'ānic principles we have quoted are just

73 *Buḥūth fi 'Ulūm al-Qur'ān al-Karīm*, pp. 218- 227.
74 The book was printed in Cairo in 1996 C.E, no publisher. It has 335 pages; the subject in question is discussed from p.292 to 353.
75 *Al-Mawsū'a al-Qur'āniyya al-Mutakhaṣṣiṣa*, pp. 82- 94.

> examples, to draw attention to this mighty aspect of the Qur'ān. They need to be researched as an independent endeavour, and the elements of each principle and the necessary premises elucidated, as well as the consequences. Then the relationships between all of these principles should be clarified, so that we can build a cognitive model. Then it should be made clear how they are to be used in various domains: politics, law, sociology, education, philosophy, worship, beliefs, *daʿwa*, and so on.

The Shaykh then suggested to our friend Shaykh Muṣṭafa ʿAbdal-Karīm Kāsib to study this issue; it became his Master Degree thesis at the department of *Tafsīr* and *Uṣūl al-Dīn*. He says in his book, *al-Mabādi' al-ʿĀmma fi'l-Qur'ān al-Karīm* (General Principles in the Noble Qur'ān)[76]:

> This is because the idea that there are Qur'ānic principles is based on extracting parts of some verses that have intelligible meanings, without consideration for the context, since these parts and sentences have clear understandable meanings that can be grasped independently from the context which they neither oppose nor contradict. An example of this is His saying - Exalted is He, ***No carrier shall carry the burden of another.***[77] Another is, ***Say: Are those who know and those who know not equal?***[78] And a third is, ***God pardons what is past.***[79] This is because the Noble Qur'ān is a

76 This is the second of two different books with the same title, the first being the one mentioned above, authored by Dr. Muḥammad al-Sayyid Badr.
77 Qur'ān, *Sūra al-Anʿām*, 164.
78 Qur'ān, *Sūra al-Zumur*, 9.
79 Qur'ān, *Sūra al-Mā'ida*, 95.

book of guidance sent down by God the Exalted so that people may be guided and find their way. This can only be achieved by means of the wealth of meanings that its expressions can bear; for the Qur'ānic expression is capable of giving many meanings all of which are intended. This is why I can see that understanding Qur'ānic sentences may have several levels:

The first level is to understand it according to the context, which is how most of the Noble Qur'ān should be understood.

The second level is to understand the Qur'ānic sentence according to its meaning independently of the context, so long as this understanding does not diverge, contradict, or invalidate the context. This is permissible for a fair number verses of the Noble Qur'ān. This is how the Qur'ānic principles came to be.

The third level is to understand the Qur'ānic sentence in a manner different from that for which it came and independent of the context. This is essentially not permissible, in fact categorically forbidden. This the manner in which the *Bāṭinīs* and other deviant sects carry out their exegesis.

Our concern here is neither the first, nor the third levels, for these are clear and require neither definition nor explanation. They are also not the subject of this study. It is the second level that I wish to clarify and explain by quoting some of the evidence for it, together with some examples, and confirming all this with scholarly opinions. This is because the second level is "to understand from the Qur'ānic sentence the meaning for which it was intended, but without recourse to the context." As such it is no different from the Qur'ānic principles. For the Qur'ānic principles are nothing but to use the Qur'ānic sentences to convey the meanings intended without consideration of the context. For instance, His saying - Exalted is He, ***God pardons what is past,***[80] is used solely for the pardon – for what was already in the past – received by those who had yet to learn of a prohibition. In its context it applied to the law concerning hunting game for those in a state of *iḥram*, the ruling regarding this and the penance, and that God – Exalted is he – has pardoned what was done before knowledge came to them that it was forbidden. However, separated from the context, it is one of the general principles of the Noble Qur'ān to the effect that legislation does not apply retroactively to the past, and therefore the law should not be applied to a past event. The principle has applications in various domains.

Such Qur'ānic sentences can have two meanings, one according to the context and the second without consideration of the context. Both are correct and intended. Another example is His saying – Exalted is

80 Qur'ān, *Sūra al-Mā'ida,* 95.

He, ***Shall the recompense for doing good be other than good?***[81] The same applies to other Qur'ānic principles.[82]

It is clear that the exegete must acquaint himself thoroughly with this kind of Qur'ānic studies and examine all aspects of every Qur'ānic expression, to be able to derive principles of polity, sociology, creed, philosophy, *da'wa*, etc… Only in this manner will he be able to give the Qur'ān the importance it deserves and allow it to guide human society in its various activities.

81 Qur'ān, *Sūra al-Raḥmān,* 60.
82 *Al-Mabādi' al-'Āmma fi'l-Qur'ān al-Karīm*, p. 10.

Divine existential laws governing human societies permeate the Book and form the subject of one of the essential sciences of the Qur'ān

HUMANITY HAS A long experience of guidance through the procession of divine envoys and heavenly messages. It has witnessed the decisive situations that divine prophets and other summoners to God went through with their communities and the patterns that God regularly imposed on mankind in the course of history. These constitute the principles controlling the change in human societies over time. When these are pursued, compiled, investigated, analyzed, and used constructively, they become the tools necessary for understanding how civilizations arise and the nature of the influences that alter human societies. This will open avenues into new kinds of knowledge and sciences that had crossed no one's mind before.

The Qur'ān persistently refers to these divine laws when explaining major historical events, when God grants victory to some people over others, causes something to occur, or destroys a community, etc. These laws are stable over time and circumstances, thus constituting a Qur'ānic phenomenon that appears on reflection to be one of the principles of Qur'ānic guidance.

Such divine laws are numerous in the Qur'ān and include the laws of complementarities, mutual checking, equilibrium, mutual acquaintance, causes and effects, testing and temptation, reward and retribution in kind, victory and firm establishment, the destruction of communities, and other laws, nearly fifty, which can be classified according to the following categories: Cosmic, psychological, social, and historical. These can form the Islamic basis for a whole system of human and sociological sciences that can be designed according to our own sources and methods of research, theorizing, deduction, and application. Shaykh 'Alī Jum'a says in his book, *Simāt al-'Aṣr* (Signs of the Times), "This kind of knowledge may lead us to formulate a science of the principles of civilization, Imām al-Shāfi'ī having formulated the science of the principles of understanding the Noble Text."[83]

Despite the Qur'ān drawing attention to these laws, calling them the "Wont of God", and repeatedly referring to them to explain various phenomena and events, the Muslims only started to give them serious systematic attention when Imām Muḥammad 'Abdu said – may God have mercy on him:

> The fact that God has pointed out to us that he has recurrent laws in His creation makes it incumbent upon us to make these the subject of a researched science, so that we may retain in the most complete manner the benefits it contains in the way of guidance and teaching. There should be among the community individuals who explain to it the laws of God in His creation, just as with other sciences and arts which the Qur'ān mentions in sum and which the scholars have

83 *Simāt al-'Aṣr*, p.36.

> explained in detail according to its instructions, such as *Tawḥīd, Uṣūl,* and *Fiqh.*[84]

However, this was only a spark and was not followed up by further efforts to investigate the matter more extensively until Shaykh Muḥammad al-Ṣādiq ʿArjūn wrote a book entitled, *Sunan Allāh fi'l-Mujtamaʿ min Khilāl al-Qur'ān* (Divine Social Laws in the Qur'ān); then others followed suit, as for example Sayyid Muḥammad Bāqir al-Ṣadr in *al-Sunan al-Tārīkhiyya fi'l-Qur'ān al-Karīm* (the Laws of History in the Noble Qur'ān), then Dr. ʿAbdal-Karīm Zaydān in *al-Sunan al-Ilāhiyya fi'l-Umam wa'l-Jamāʿāt wa'l-Afrād fi'l-Sharīʿa al-Islāmiyya* (Divine Laws of Communities, Social Groups and Individuals in Islamic Law) and Dr. Muṣṭafa al-Shakʿa in *al-Sunan al-Ilāhiyya fī Riḥāb al-Qur'ān al-Karīm* (Divine Laws in the Noble Qur'ān), followed by Muḥammad Hayshūr in *Sunan al-Qur'ān fī Qiyām al-Ḥaḍārāt wa Suqūtihā* (Qur'ānic Laws of the Rise and Fall of Civilizations), Dr. Majdī Muḥammad ʿĀshūr in *al-Sunan al-Ilāhiyya fi'l-Umam wa'l-Afrād fi'l-Qur'ān al-Karīm, Uṣūl wa Ḍawābiṭ,* (Divine Laws of Communities and Individuals in the Noble Qur'ān: Principles and Definitions) and Dr. Sayf ʿAbdal-Fattāḥ in *Madkhal al-Qiyam* (Introduction to Values).

There is no doubt that one of the most important duties of the exegete is to acquaint himself with this science and follow up the investigations of those who study it and their incursions into psychology, sociology, the philosophy of history, and other scientific domains. This is because it opens wide the doors to understanding the purposes of the Qur'ān. Imām Muḥammad ʿAbdu considered this science one of the things without which the higher levels of exegesis cannot be reached. He says in his introduction to *Tafsīr*

---

84 *Al-Aʿmāl al-Kāmila li'l-Shaykh Muḥammad ʿAbdu,* 5:95.

al-Manār (Al-Manār Commentary):

> The third is knowledge of the human condition. God has sent down this book, making it the last one and explaining in it much that had not been explained in previous books. He explains much of the conditions of people, their characters, and the divine laws governing them, and relates to us the most excellent narrations about previous communities and how his laws applied to them. Therefore, he who studies this Book must study the condition of human beings in their various stages and changes, the causes for the differences in their conditions, whether in matters of strength or weakness, knowledge or ignorance, faith or disbelief; and also knowledge of the universe with its higher and lower worlds. This requires many arts, among the most important of which is history in all its categories.

He also says:

> I cannot understand how someone can comment on His saying – Exalted is He, ***The people were one community, then God sent the Envoys with good news and warnings,***[85] when ignorant of the conditions of the human race, how they were united and then separated, what this first unity meant and whether it was beneficial or harmful, and what happened when the Prophets were sent among them.[86]

85 Qur'ān, *Sūra al-Baqara,* 213.
86 *Tafsīr al-Manār*, 1/20.

The Science of Qur'ānic Purposes, one of the most important tools of the exegete

THE QUR'ĀN IS a venerable divine book intended to include the essence of guidance for mankind and contain great purposes and sublime goals. It reveals in all their dimensions the great issues that have been and remain of crucial importance to mankind such as Divinity, Revelation, Prophecy, guidance, matchlessness, Sacred Law, human values, organization, good manners and courtesy, the principles guiding human societies, the growth and purification of the soul, how to create civilization and prosperity on earth, the rights of the other worlds[87], and relations among nations.

The Qur'ān is undoubtedly much richer than the Law, for the latter is but one among its many subjects, which makes it imperative to have a science called the Science of Qur'ānic Purposes that researches and records these, classifies them in superimposed levels, deduces the rules governing each level, and relates them to every aspect of life and thought. Thus will Qur'ānic purposes, both primary and secondary, become clear, as will the far-reaching aims which promote the issue of guidance in the souls, hearts, and minds of the people and across the nations.

87 Islam provides a complete set of instructions designed to preserve not only human rights, but the rights of animals, plants, and the environment in general, and also those of the "other worlds" which include invisible worlds such as those of the Jinn and the angels. These instructions lead to the observance of appropriate courtesy and regulate interaction to prevent mutual harm.

There is a difference between the Science of Qur'ānic Purposes and that of the Purposes of the Law, for the first is general while the second is particular; for every purpose of the Sacred Law is also by the same token a purpose of the Qur'ān, but there are other purposes in the Qur'ān that are unrelated to the Law, such as for example good manners, values, and beliefs.

The Science of Purposes of the Law was studied by the *Uṣūlīs*. Earlier scholars such as Imām al-Ḥaramayn in *al-Burhān* and Imām al-Ghazālī in *Shifā' al-Ghalīl* have given precious glimpses of their thoughts on the matter. These few sentences were later to constitute the basis of that science. Then this science gradually came of age at the hand of those who are considered its real founders, the first being the Independent Imām al-ʿIzz ibn ʿAbdal-Salām in *Qawāʿid al-Aḥkām fi Maṣāliḥ al-Anām* (The Foundations of the Regulations of the Interests of the People), Imām *al-Qarāfī* in *al-Furūq* (The Differences), followed by Imām al-Shāṭibī with *Al-Muwāfaqāt* (The Concordances). Finally, among the latecomers are al-Ṭāhir ibn ʿĀshūr who, with *Maqāsid al-Sharīʿa al-Islāmiyya* (Purposes of Islamic Law), separated this science from the science of *Uṣūl,* turning it into an independent science. Then came Dr. Sayf al-Dīn ʿAbdal-Fattāḥ with *Madkhal al-Qiyam* (Introduction to Values), followed by tens of other scholars, until the science of *Maqāsid al-Sharīʿa* reached a high level of maturity and precision.

The early exegetes expressed these Qur'ānic purposes in a summary manner, stating that Revelation includes three things: *Tawḥīd*, Law, and narratives, as stated for example by Ibn Ḥajar in *Fatḥ al-Bārī.*[88] It is perhaps Imām al-Ghazālī who first discussed in more detail the purposes of the Qur'ān. In *Jawāhir al-Qur'ān* (Jewels of the Qur'ān) he

88 *Fatḥ al-Bārī*, 8: 719.

stated that these were six, three essential and three complementary. He says:

> As for the three essential ones, they are to inform of Him to whom it calls, of the straight path that must be followed to reach Him, and what happens when He is reached. As for the three complementary ones, the first is to inform of the states of those who respond to the summons, and the grace with which God treats them, the secret and purpose of this being to arouse yearning and desire. It is also to inform of the states of those who turn back and refuse to respond, and how God will subdue and severely punish them. Its secret and purpose is to get them to heed the lesson and put fear into them. The second is to narrate the stories of the rejecters, and then expose their ignorance and shameful behaviour by means of debate and telling arguments. Its purpose is, as far as the side aligned with error is concerned, exposure and dissuasion; while for the side aligned with the truth it is clarification, confirmation and victory. The third is to inform of how the stations that lie on the road are caused to flourish, and how to gather provision, prepare and be ready. These are six divisions.[89]

He then goes on to discuss these divisions in details; the whole book is centred on this subject.

One is given to wonder how Imām Suyūṭī, despite his passion for multiplying and varying the sciences of the Qur'ān, can quote Imām

89 *Jawāhir al-Qur'ān*, p. 23.

Ghazālī so many times in *al-Itqān* without being alerted to the need to make this an independent science.

In his biography of Imām Fayrūzabādī, author of the well known dictionary *al-Qāmūs al-Muḥīṭ*, Imām Sakhāwī states that among his books is one entitled *al-Durr al-Naẓīm al-Murshid ilā Maqāsid al-Qur'ān al-Karīm* (The Array of Pearls: A Guide to the Purposes of the Noble Qur'ān).[90] This book seems never to have been printed. I have not managed to find it in manuscript form or even find out what its contents are, but it seems to be a very important book on the subject. The author's biographer quotes passages from it to the effect that there are nine dimensions to the Qur'ān: The permitted and the prohibited, the precise and the ambiguous, good news and warnings, stories, lessons, and similitudes. Then I came upon Imām Shawkānī's following words in *Irshād al-Thiqāt* (Guidance for the Trustworthy):

> As for the purposes of the Noble Qur'ān that are reiterated therein accompanied with both observational and rational evidence, and to which it attracts attention in all its *sūras* and most of its stories and examples, they are three. They are only recognized by him who is capable of complete understanding, deliberate meditation, rich imagination and superior reflection. The first purpose is to prove *Tawḥīd*, the second to prove the life-to-come, and the third to prove the missions of the Prophets."[91]

Other than what has just been quoted, I am not aware of any other

---

90 Sakhāwī, *al-Ḍaw' al-Lāmi' fī A'yān al-Qarn al-Tāsi'*, 10: 81.
91 *Irshād al-Thiqāt ilā Ittifāq al-Sharā'i' 'alā Ithbāt al-Tawḥīd wa'l-Ma'ād wa'l-Nubuwwāt*, p. 3.

writings concerning this important science of the Qur'ān.

We can say that the Qur'ān has major purposes among which are:

The questions of Divinity, by which are meant the questions of *Tawḥīd*, the Attributes of the Real, and that which is necessary, impossible, or possible for Him.

The question of what God desires for His creation, for instance that He desires for us ease, to lighten our burden, to make things clear to us, and to inform us that He promises us His forgiveness and favour. These are different from the subjects of *Tawḥīd* and Sacred law on the one hand, while on the other the Qur'ān explicitly states that they constitute part of what God desires for us. This then is a major Qur'ānic purpose that must be studied in depth.

The question of Revelation, and that it is the criterion separating those who accept from those who reject it. He says – Exalted is He, ***Say, he who is the enemy of Jibrīl, He has sent him down upon your heart, with God's permission, to confirm that which came before it, a guidance and good news for the believers. He who is an enemy of God, His angels, His Envoys, Jibrīl, and Mikāl, God is the enemy of the disbelievers. We have sent down upon you clear signs and only the corrupt disbelieve it.***[92]

Arraying and authenticating the evidence for Revelation is a major Qur'ānic purpose upon which other major questions depend. This is why the Qur'ān emphasises its importance and establishes its foundations, and this is why it defends Jibrīl in the above mentioned

92 Qur'ān, *Sūra al-Baqara,* 97-99.

passage of *Sūra al-Baqara* and blames the previous communities for tampering with Revelation, even while providing assurances that the Qur'ān is to be divinely preserved from any such tampering.

Similar statements can be made concerning the questions of Prophecy, guidance, matchlessness, Sacred Law, values, organizational systems, good manners, guiding principles for human societies, the growth and purification of the human soul, civilization and prosperity on earth, the rights of the other worlds, relations between nations, and other subjects that must be studied separately. The exegete has to be well acquainted with all this and be constantly aware of these purposes, so that he may be able to grasp how examples are given for it, stories told, news related, and *sūras* revealed. Only then will he be able to use them appropriately.

Effect of the Science of Derivatives on understanding the text

DERIVATION[93] IS ONE of the most important linguistic sciences, as well as one of the most critical in understanding certain word structures; one that reveals the richness of the Arabic language. It is based on grasping the essential meaning of the root word, then following it through every possible derivative, or alternatively on compiling all the words that share a similarity of meaning, and then extracting from them the essential meaning which constitutes the centre they revolve around. One can also derive from the same root a number of forms to express subtle differences between interrelated meanings, so that they will have in common the same essential meaning, but with differences brought about by the context and manner in which the word is used.

This science is quite immense, quite subtle, but also very precise, and the books discussing it are innumerable. Here we are concerned with one kind of derivation only, which has received numerous names by various scholars. Rāzī, for example calls it the Greater Derivation *(al-Ishtiqāq al-Akbar)* in *Mafātīḥ al-Ghayb*, in which he was followed by Muḥammad Rāghib Bāshā in his *Safīna*, then Ṣiddīq Ḥasan Khān in *al-'Alam al-Khaffāq min 'Ilm al-Ishtiqāq* (The Flapping Standard in the Science of Derivation). Ibn Ginnī on the other hand called it the

93 Derivation is the approximate equivalent of Etymology.

Small Derivation (*al-Ishtiqāq al-Saghīr)* in *al-Khaṣā'iṣ* and Shawkānī follows suit in *Nuzhat'al-Aḥdāq fī'Ilm al-Ishtiqāq* (Promenade of the Pupils of the Eye in the Science of Derivation). 'Abdallāh Amīn calls it *al-Ishtiqāq al-Kibār* and also *al-Qalb al-Lughawī*[94]. These different appellations refer but to a single science. I am drawing your attention to this so that you may be able to identify it under its various names in various works. To follow is a brief introduction to it.

'Abdallāh Amīn writes in *al-Ishtiqāq* (Derivation),

> "*al-Ishtiqāq al-Kibār* is to derive one word from another by changing the order of some of its letters. The result will be two words similar in meaning and composed of the same letters, but in different order. This kind of derivation is called *Qalb Lughawī*, to differentiate it from it from the *Qalb sarfī I'lālī* which is to replace one vowel with another. Linguistic derivation being one among a number of components of the Science of Derivation, I choose to call it *al-Qalb al-Ishtiqāqī*. It occurs most often in three letters words, in two forms of the same root, such as *Jadhabahu* and *Jabadhahu*, when one pulls another to him; and *shajja ra'sah* and *jasha* when he cracks his head."[95]

This is how it is actually put to work. Rāzī says in *al-Tafsīr al-Kabīr:*

> First issue: Know that the most perfect way to define the meaning of words is that of *Ishtiqāq* or Derivation, which is of two kinds: Smaller and Greater. The Smaller Derivation or *Ishtiqāq Asghar* is to derive past

94 The literal meaning of *Qalb Lughawī* is: linguistic reversal.
95 *Al-Ishtiqāq*, p. 2.

and future forms from the root verb, or active and passive participles. As for the Greater Derivation or *Ishtiqāq Akbar*, it comes from the fact that words are composed of letters which are of necessity capable of being shifted around. We say: The first level is when the word is made of two letters, which makes it capable of only two kinds of transformation, as in: *man* and *nam*[96]. Then there is the level when it is made of three letters, as in *ḥamd*. This word is capable of six kinds of transformation, for each of the three letters can be positioned at the beginning of the word, and for each of these three possibilities the other two letters can be in two ways, so that three is multiplied by two to give six. These are the transformations a three lettered word is capable of. Following this there is the degree of the four lettered word, as in *ʿaqrab* (*ʿaqrab*) and *thaʿlab* (*thaʿlab*). It is capable of accepting twenty four kinds of transformation, for each of the four letters can be positioned at the beginning of the word, and for each of these four possibilities the remaining three letters can be arranged in six different orders. Four by six gives twenty four forms. Then there is the five lettered word such as *safarjal*, which accepts one hundred and twenty kinds of transformation, for each of these five words may be positioned at the beginning of the word, then for each of these possibilities the letters can be arranged in twenty four different orders, and five by twenty four is a hundred and twenty.

---

96 The vowels *a, i* and *u* are not written in Arabic, so that *man* is two letters *mn*, and *ḥamd* three letters *ḥmd*.

He goes on to say:

> Second issue: Know that the status of the Smaller Derivation or *Ishtiqāq Aṣghar* is familiar and easy to understand. On the other hand, the Greater Derivation or *Ishtiqāq Akbar* is more difficult to study and it seems that it can be studied only as far as three lettered words go. As for four and five lettered ones, the derivations are too numerous, most of them are never used, so that it can be done only on rare occasions. Even three lettered words can rarely be meaningful in all their possible transformations; more usually some forms are used and some not. The maximum one can aim for in investigating the meaning of words in linguistic studies is to investigate the forms that are actually in use.[97]

The expert linguist Aḥmad Fāris al-Shidyāq carefully collected all the words where shifting and transformation had occurred, together with their synonyms.

Here is an example of how an analysis of word derivation can be carried out on a word from the Qur'ān. This will clarify for you the benefits of this noble science and its effect in understanding of the full the intended meanings of the Qur'ān, some of which may have been hidden behind the form of the word, which at the same time subtly reveals the intended meaning by the very manner in which it is derived. Here the subtle indication takes the role of the explicit declaration. We shall take the root *k l m* for an example. This root is capable of accepting six forms, as shown above: *k l m, k m l, l k m, l m k, m k l, m l k*. The Arabs have used five of these and ignored the

97 *Al-Tafsīr al-Kabīr*, 1; 24.

sixth, which is *l m k*.

The author of *al-ʿAlam al-Khaffāq* says:

> The meaning shared by all these forms indicates harsh power, since *kalm* means wound, indicating harshness. *Kulām* is rough ground, for its strength and hardness. *Kalīm* is a wounded man. *Kamula, kāmil, kamīl*, all mean completion, the first being the verb, the second and third being adjectives. This is because a complete thing is more powerful and hard than an incomplete thing. *Lakama* means to punch and cause pain; the harsh power in this is obvious. We say: *Makulat al-bi'r*[98] when the water of the well dwindles. *Bi'r makūl*, is a well with little water in it. Here the meaning comes from the sides of the well which when it goes dry become rough and harsh. Angels are called *malak* because of their might and power.[99]

According to this, the exegete can expand on the meaning of *malak*. Angels are a noble kind of created beings that the Qur'ān mentions, detailing some of their attributes, while passing others over in silence. The derivative form of the word itself indicates might and power. Thus the origin of the term *malak* is might, so that might governs the attributes of angels. They neither eat, nor drink. They need no sleep and are capable of praising their Lord night and day unrelentingly. These are attributes of great strength. Some of them are the keepers of Hell, mighty and extremely harsh. Together with this they are entirely submitted to God, fear him greatly, and do nothing but what they are commanded to do. As they carry the

---

98 *Bi'r* means well.
99 *Al-ʿAlam al-Khaffāq*, p. 45.

divine throne, they sing the praises of their Lord and ask forgiveness for the believers. All this directs the exegete's attention toward the Qur'ān's use of the angels to clarify the concept of divine might and of the total submission of the worlds to Him. Let us examine the following passage for example, ***When you said to the believers, "Is it not sufficient for you that God should reinforce you with three thousand angels sent down upon you? Yes! If you are patient and God-fearing and they come at you right now, God will reinforce you with five thousand angels wearing their marks. God only made it to be good news for, that your hearts might find tranquility in it. Assistance is only from God, the August, the Wise.***[100] Such perception of the angels as mighty and harsh will allow the exegete to see how awesome in effect was reinforcing the Muslims with three then five thousand angels, and how this was a tremendous event designed to shake the enemies' hearts with fear. It also allows him to understand the true impact of the good news that they were about to join the ranks of the Muslim army. In this manner will we understand why the Qur'ān follows this immediately with mentioning tranquility of the heart, then cutting off a section of the disbelievers, thwarting them and turning them on their tracks, confounded.[101] This would have been the natural consequence of sending down a single angel, so how much more with thousands of them?

This also draws attention to the difference in concept with the usual image of the angel in Western culture, where the angels are seen as entirely subtle, gentle, and peaceful creatures. Both the Qur'ānic description and adequate understanding of the deeper meanings of the word go against this image. Thus when translating the meanings

---

100 Qur'ān, *Sūra Āl-'Imrān*, 124-126.

101 The next verse says, ***That He might cut off a section of the disbelievers or thwart them, so that they are sent back on their tracks, confounded.***

of the Qur'ān it should be borne in mind that the word angel should be explained in such a manner as to bring out these dimensions.

Thus also do the specific attributes of Jibrīl become clear. The Real describes him as, ***Taught by one of mighty powers. Extremely powerful, he stood poised.***[102] His specific attribute, however, is not simply power, for all angels are by definition powerful, but extreme power. This is why the Qur'ānic expression here ***Extremely powerful*** is seen to be very precise, for it indicates a higher than ordinary level of power. This also sheds lights on His saying again about Jibrīl, ***It is but the utterance of a noble messenger, powerful, with the Lord of the Throne secure.***[103] Here on the other hand he is described as powerful, without further qualification, for the word *malak* that denotes power is not mentioned, and one may not be able to distinguish whether it is the Prophet or the angel that is meant, since the angel is here called messenger. The eloquent Arab, aware of the original meaning *malak*, will understand that it is Jibrīl that is meant here and not the Prophet. Thus does the word ***powerful*** in this context serve to convey the meaning of ***angel***. There was no need to say ***extremely powerful*** in *Sūra al-Takwīr* because the quality of Jibrīl that needs to be emphasized there is his secure position near the Lord of the Throne, contrary to *Sūra al-Najm* where the quality emphasized was the mighty power of the angel. It would have added nothing to the meaning to describe him as ***extremely powerful*** since it is clear that he is the one meant by the verse. The context in *Sūra al-Najm* is clear: there is one who receives Revelation, one who communicates Revelation, and One who reveals. He says, ***Your companion has not strayed, neither was he misled, nor does he speak out of caprice; it is but revelation communicated, taught by one of mighty powers, extremely***

102 Qur'ān, *Sūra al-Najm,* 5,6.
103 Qur'ān, *Sūra al-Takwīr,* 19, 20.

powerful, he stood poised.[104] He mentions the Prophet, states that his words are also Revelation, then moves on to the description of him who communicates Revelation to him, so that it becomes clear that now the one meant is an angel, which in itself suggests power, so that to add that this power is extreme would be evidently appropriate.

Once we familiarize ourselves with meditating upon Qur'ānic words in this manner, vast new horizons open up inviting us to comprehend the vast concepts intended by the Qur'ān. 'Abdallāh Amīn says, "This kind of derivation, when exploited to the full, supplies the language with excellent resources."[105] I say: this is because words will then open up their dimensions to us and each will reveal its depths, which is clearly of utmost importance in understanding the Qur'ān.

Dr. 'Awdat'Allāh Manī' al-Qaysī has gone a great distance toward applying the rules of *Ishtiqāq* in his very important book, *Sirr al-I'jāz fī Tanawwu' al-Ṣiyagh al-Mushtaqqa min Aṣl Lughawī Wāḥid fi'l-Qur'ān* (The Secret of the Inimitable Variety of Derivatives from a Single Linguistic Origin in the Qur'ān).

With this we come to the conclusion of our book. We ask God to open the doors of understanding His Noble Book for us and grant us His support, guidance and wisdom. We praise and thank Him for His gracious favours and generous assistance.

May God bless our master Muḥammad, his family and companions, and grant them peace.

---

104 Qur'ān, *Sūra al-Najm,* 5,6.
105 *Al-Ishtiqāq,* p. 2.